The Wish-Fulfilling Jewel

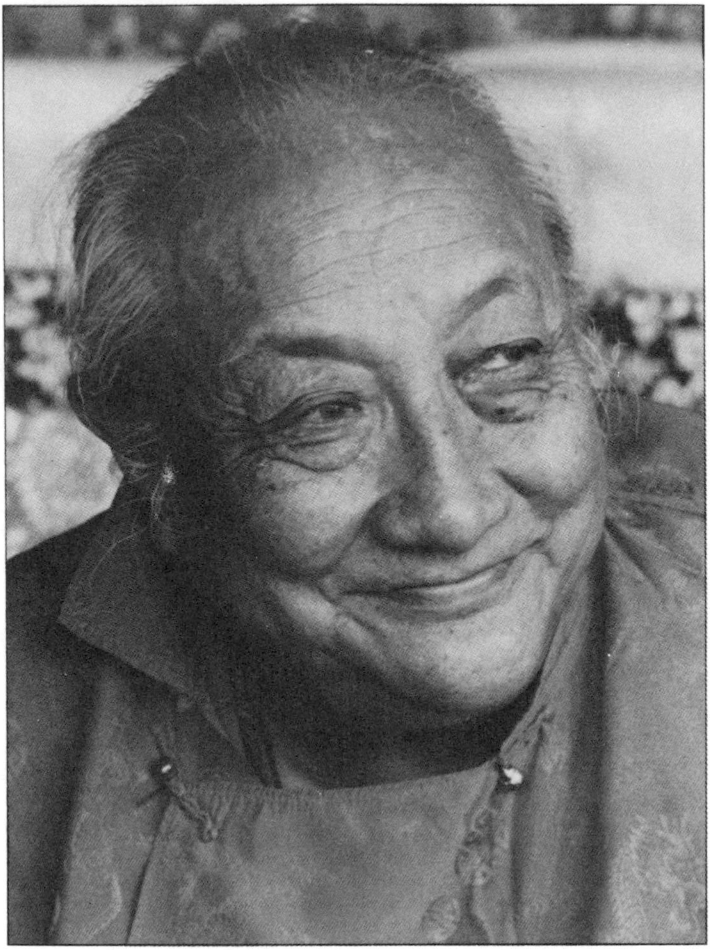

His Holiness Khyentse Rinpoche

The Wish-Fulfilling Jewel

THE PRACTICE OF GURU YOGA ACCORDING TO THE LONGCHEN NYINGTHIG TRADITION

Dilgo Khyentse

Translated from the Tibetan by
Könchog Tenzin

SHAMBHALA
Boston & London
1994

Shambhala Publications, Inc.
Horticultural Hall
300 Massachusetts Avenue
Boston, MA 02115

9 8 7 6 5 4 3 2 1

Printed in the United States of America on acid-free paper. ♾

Distributed in the United States by Random House and in Canada by Random House of Canada Ltd.

Library of Congress Cataloging-in-Publication Data

Rab-gsal-zla-ba, Dil-mgo Mkhyen-brtsc, 1910–
The wish-fulfilling jewel: the practice of guru yoga according to the Longchen Nyingthig / Dilgo Khyentse: translated from the Tibetan by Könchog Tenzin.
p. cm.
ISBN 1-57062-052-0 (pbk.)
1. Guru worship (Rite)—Buddhism. 2. Buddhism—China—Tibet. I. Title
BQ7699.G87R83 1988 87-32250
294.3'61—dc19 CIP

Contents

The Wish-Fulfilling Jewel

Introduction

The teachings found here concern a fundamental and most precious practice known as guru yoga. The words *guru yoga* mean "union with the nature of the guru," and in this practice we are given methods by which we can blend our own minds with the enlightened mind of the guru.

It is said that all the buddhas of the three times—those of the past and the present and those to come—achieve buddhahood through reliance on a spiritual teacher. The essence of reliance on a teacher is unceasing devotion, and the most effective means of generating and sustaining unwavering devotion is precisely the practice of guru yoga. Through this practice, devotion to the teacher takes firm root within us and eventually grows to pervade our entire being. It protects our practice from obstacles and ensures progress on the path. Devotion to the teacher is thus the core of all our spiritual practice, regardless of the particular stages of the path we cultivate. For these reasons, guru yoga is considered the most vital and necessary of all practices and is in itself the surest and fastest way to reach the goal of enlightenment.

Why is the blending of our mind with the guru's mind such an essential practice? Although the guru at first may appear to us in ordinary human form and although he may at first appear to behave in an ordinary human way, his mind really is inseparable in nature from the mind of the

Buddha. The qualities of the guru differ in no way from those of a perfectly enlightened buddha.

Actually, the only difference between the guru and the buddhas is that his kindness exceeds that of all the enlightened ones of the past. For instance, Buddha Śākyamuni left this world over two thousand years ago, while other buddhas, such as Amitābha and Vajrasattva, are dwelling in their respective buddha-fields. They are perfectly enlightened buddhas, but we can neither meet them face to face nor hear their teachings, because our minds are now thick with obscuration. Our guru, on the other hand, has come into this world at this time. We can meet him and receive from him the precious instructions that will lead us out of the mire of *saṃsāra*[1] to enlightenment. So, although our guru is equal to all the buddhas in his qualities, he exceeds them in his kindness.

The specific text that we will use and explain here is drawn from the Longchen Nyingthig, the profound and extensive cycle of teachings revealed by the great saint and *tertön*,[2] Rigdzin Jigme Lingpa,[3] whose name means "Fearless Holder of Awareness." He is also known as Khyentse Öser, which means "Light Rays of Wisdom and Love," a name given to him in visions. Longchen Nyingthig means "Heart Essence of the Great Expanse."

At this point, it is appropriate to offer an account of the origin of the Longchen Nyingthig and in this way strengthen our confidence in the authenticity of these teachings. According to Jigme Lingpa himself, the teachings came to him in the following way:

> As the fruit of my fervent prayers in countless lives never to be separate from the compassion and blessing of Urgyen,[4] the king of the dharma, and

of his consort, the *ḍākinī* Yeshe Tsogyal,[5] I was able to apprehend the all-pervasive suffering of *saṃsāra*. At this I experienced great sadness and, the urge to free myself from cyclic existence having arisen within me, I went to Palri Thekchogling[6] intending to spend three years in strenuous and one-pointed spiritual practice.

One morning at dawn, as I was engaged in the recitation of the hundred peaceful and wrathful deities,[7] an intense feeling of renunciation and weariness with *saṃsāra* surged up within my mind. At that moment my surroundings became filled with great light, and Urgyen, the dharma king, with Rigdzin Jampal She-nyen[8] and many others arrayed around him, appeared in the sky in front of me. After some time they dissolved into me, and my mind became empty of all ordinary thought. All traces of clinging to the experiences of meditation vanished, all karmic energies fell under my control, and the fictitious fortress of appearances collapsed. Ordinary perceptions of this life faded completely from my mind and, as if emerging into a new life, I entered and remained in a state in which I remembered fully having been Ngari Panchen Pema Wangyal.[9]

Not long after this, I dreamed I was in an unfamiliar place that was said to be the celestial field "Spontaneous Accomplishment of All Wishes." There I saw, riding on a dragon, Dorje Drolö[10] standing, moving, formidable yet insubstantial as if made of rainbow light. A monk, who I thought was the protector Damchen Dorje Lekpa,[11] said, "This is the deity to whom the following verse refers: '*Urgyen and the Yidam*[12] *are indissociable. There is no doubt that the son will receive the father's treasure.*'" He said this and everything vanished.

Several days passed. Then, during the evening of the twenty-fifth day of the tenth month of the Female Fire Ox year [1757], a fiery devotion toward the great master Guru Padmasambhava arose within me, filling my eyes with tears. Memories from a remote past flashed across my mind, and with overwhelming sadness I thought, "Here in this land of red-faced men, people live mired in hatred, lust, and ignorance, wallowing in nothing but the most vicious of actions. There is nothing left but a pale shadow of the teachings, and I myself feel like an orphan abandoned in the wilderness. You, compassionate protector, greater than any other buddha, have left this land and gone to the Copper-Colored Mountain.[13] Will I ever be able to meet you?"

Tormented by sorrow, I wept. Just at that moment, the air around me became filled with light, and suddenly, standing before me, I beheld a beautiful white snow lioness. I took my seat on her back and we leaped into the limitless immensity of the sky. Soon we arrived at Jarungkhashor,[14] the great stupa of Nepal. There, on the eastern side of the stupa, stood the ḍākinī[15] of the *dharmakāya* wisdom.

She handed me a sealed flat wooden casket, and said:

> For those with pure perception,
> You are King Trisong Detsen.[16]
> For those whose perception is less pure,

You are Senge Repa, the cotton-clad Lion Yogi.
Here is the Heart Treasure of Samantabhadra,[17]
The Symbol of the infinite mind of the Vidyādhara Padma,
The great secret treasure of the ḍākinīs.

Having spoken thus, she vanished, leaving me quite shaken. Then, filled with great joy, I opened the casket. Within, I found five scrolls of yellow parchment and seven small crystals the size of a pea. As I unrolled the largest of the scrolls, the air was suffused with an indescribable fragrance of medicinal herbs and camphor, and my entire being seemed to quiver with the mystery of it. A thought, unbidden, made itself clear in my mind: "Rāhula[18] protects this treasure. It is extremely powerful and should be approached with great caution." With reverence and awe I slowly unfurled the scroll. It bore the image of a stupa completely covered with ḍākinī script, seemingly beyond the reach of human understanding. Unable to decipher it, I began to roll the parchment closed when, suddenly, like a mirage, the stupa disappeared and the ḍākinī script dissolved and reformed into Tibetan script. It was a text on the Great Compassionate One.[19] This entire text arose as clearly as if it were an image in a mirror. After some time it again grew difficult to read, becoming progressively less clear. . . .

In this and other related visions, Jigme Lingpa opened other scrolls and, eventually, having swallowed the remaining ones as instructed by a ḍākinī, he experienced boundless realization of the bliss-awareness void.

Under the direction of his guru, he kept these teachings secret for seven years. Then, in the course of a three-year retreat at Chimphu, in the mountains above Samye,[20] he had three visions of Kunkhyen Longchen Rabjam,[21] the emanation of Vimalamitra,[22] who himself had attained the level of the primordial buddha Samantabhadra, and their minds merged into one. In these visions, Longchen Rabjam urged Jigme Lingpa to disclose his visionary treasures and teach them to sentient beings.

In accordance with the prophecy, on the tenth day of the Monkey month of the Male Wood-Monkey year [1764], while he was performing the invitation section of an abundant feast offering, Guru Padmasambhava, in full splendor and surrounded by a cloudlike retinue of ḍākas and ḍākinīs, appeared in the sky. Guru Rinpoche then blessed him and dispelled all obstacles hindering the propagation and establishment of these teachings.

Shortly after this, although Jigme Lingpa had never given anyone the slightest hint that he was in possession of such visionary teaching, he was approached by Drati Rikpe Dorje, the mad yogi of Kongpo,[23] who without hesitation requested the teachings. Acceding to these entreaties, he gradually unfolded them, bestowing on his disciples all the initiations and explanations for the practice of these profound treasures.

The cycle of the Longchen Nyingthig is composed of many sections. It includes the preliminary and main practices, the development and completion stages, and, most important, the practice of Ati Yoga, or the Great Perfection.[24] It thus constitutes a complete path to enlightenment.

Guru Yoga

Guru yoga, the union with the nature of the guru, forms the foundation for all practices, and there are many different techniques for its practice. Within guru yoga there are outer, inner, secret, and most secret methods. The text at hand explains the outer method, which, briefly, is to visualize the guru dwelling above our head and to pray to him ardently, with fierce devotion.

The inner method is to realize, through the practice, that our own body, speech, and mind are inseparable from the wisdom body, speech, and mind of the guru. In the Longchen Nyingthig cycle, the inner method is a Guru Rinpoche *sādhana* called the Rigdzin Düpa, or the Gathering of the Awareness Holders.

The secret method is to meditate upon the guru in his *sambhogakāya* form, the body of divine enjoyment, which in this cycle is the practice of Guru Rinpoche in the form of Chenrezik and is called the Dugngel Rangdrol, or Self-Liberation of Suffering.

The most secret method introduces us to the natural state of awareness and here involves the visualization of Kunkhyen Longchenpa with the primordial Buddha Samantabhadra in his heart. This most secret sādhana is called the Thigle Gyachen, or Sealed Quintessence.

On the absolute level, the teacher is one with the very nature of our own mind, which is itself the essence of buddhahood, the *tathāgatagarbha*. What, then, is the method for realization of this absolute teacher? Through the outer or relative teacher and his pith instructions, we can bring ourselves to the realization of the inner or absolute teacher, which is awareness itself. The foundation and thus the very basis for the accomplishment of this realization is the present guru yoga, which belongs to the outer method and is classified technically as a part of the preliminary practices. Since the actual heart of all other stages and practices is precisely this guru yoga, one would be quite mistaken to think of it as just a preliminary practice and therefore unimportant. Rather, we should realize that if we practice this guru yoga continuously throughout our entire life, then all the blessings of Guru Rinpoche himself will easily enter our being.

Essentially, the practice is to remember the guru in all our activities, whether in meditation or in postmeditation periods. Thus, the actual sādhana does not require that we remain within the boundaries of a retreat, and it is appropriate for all occasions and circumstances, as well as for practitioners of all levels.

Since the mind dwells within the body, it is important to assume a proper body posture. When the trunk and spine are held in an upright position, the channels[25] become straight and the mind becomes clear. If we lounge about in a completely careless manner, it will be quite difficult for concentration, or samādhi, to be born properly within us. Therefore, we should sit in the seven-point posture[26] called the Vairocana posture.

This practice of guru yoga is meant to generate extraordinary devotion, the fervent devotion that allows us to see the guru as in no way different from Lord Buddha himself. If one sees the teacher merely as an ordinary being, then one will receive only the "blessings" of ordinary beings; if one sees him as an *arhat* or *pratyekabuddha* or *śrāvaka,* then one will receive the corresponding blessings; if one sees the teacher as a bodhisattva, one will receive the blessings of the bodhisattvas. If, however, one can see the teacher as a buddha, then one will receive the blessings of the buddhas.

There is no buddha who became enlightened without having relied upon a spiritual teacher. So to be able to practice genuine dharma one must first search for a fully realized master and attend him with total confidence. As it is said in the sutras: "It is through faith alone that one can realize the absolute nature." Without faith, even if one knows all the sections of the teachings by heart, it is of no use. This is particularly true for a practitioner of the Vajrayāna.

How, then, should we generate this fervent devotion? At present, the guru has assumed a human form and resembles an ordinary person, but his mind is unwaveringly settled in wisdom. If we could know his innermost mind, we would discover that, through his having been able to discard all defects and to realize all there is to be realized, he is equal in all aspects and qualities to a perfectly enlightened buddha. This discovery is the source of deep and genuine devotion.

He is like a great ship for beings to cross the perilous ocean of existence, an unerring captain who guides them to the dry land of liberation, a rain that extinguishes the fire of the passions, a bright sun and moon that dispel the darkness of ignorance, a firm ground that can bear the weight of both good and bad, a wish-fulfilling tree that bestows temporal happiness and ultimate bliss, a treasury of vast and deep instructions, a wish-fulfilling jewel granting all the qualities of realization, a father and a mother giving their love equally to all sentient beings, a great river of compassion, a mountain rising above worldly concerns unshaken by the winds of emotions, and a great cloud filled with rain to soothe the torments of the passions. In brief, he is the equal of all the buddhas. To make any connection with him, whether through seeing him, hearing his voice, remembering him, or being touched by his hand, will lead us toward liberation. To have full confidence in him is the sure way to progress toward enlightenment. The warmth of his wisdom and compassion will melt the ore of our being and release the gold of the buddha-nature within.

Whether or not we achieve realization depends entirely upon our devotion to the guru. For instance, Tilopa did not ask, and Dorje Chang did not offer, a single word of teaching, yet Tilopa was liberated. This was due simply to the strength of Tilopa's devotion. If the disciple has the ring of faith and devotion, then the hook of the guru's wisdom and compassion will pull him swiftly to the land of liberation. As it is said:

> When the sun of fierce devotion shines
> On the snow mountain of the guru's four *kāya*s,
> The stream of blessings will pour down.
> Therefore, strive to generate devotion in your mind.

And also:

> To remember the guru for a single instant
> Is infinitely greater than to meditate
> For a million *kalpa*s on a hundred thousand deities.

Though the boundless compassion of Amitābha and Vajrasattva never forsakes us, due to our obscurations we cannot meet them face to face. Our own teacher, however, is kinder than all the buddhas because we can now, in this very life, meet him in person and receive from him the precious instructions. The great teacher Patrul Rinpoche used a simple analogy: not all rich people in the world are equally kind. The kindest help poor people who have neither food nor sustenance. Even if we were to meet all the buddhas in their paradises, we would not receive from them any teachings or instructions more extraordinary or more profound than those given us by our own teacher, nor would we, through some miracle, be lifted up from the lower realms and established in enlightenment by them the way an aircraft lifts us into the sky.

We do not necessarily need to receive a great number of different instructions to achieve enlightenment. In fact, the eighty-four *mahāsiddha*s of India achieved realization and complete buddhahood by meditating upon four verses of teaching. They did not go through a vast assortment of instructions, but practiced one-pointedly the very one they received.

In the same way, if when meeting the guru we feel complete confidence and engender strong devotion toward him, we possess the main elements to progress along the path. But if we lack confidence and fervent devotion, if we are unable to perceive the guru as the Buddha, then, though we may have collected a multitude of instructions, not only will we find progress impossible, but we risk falling into extreme deviations as did the monk Lekpe Karma, or "Good Star."

Lekpe Karma had spent most of his life near Lord Buddha and during that time had received an abundance of teachings. With his unfailing memory he had learned by heart the whole of the Tripiṭaka. Yet, because he lacked faith and had negative views toward Buddha Śākyamuni, he believed that the Buddha's deeds and teachings were no more than schemes designed to fool people. Because of this he cut himself off from all blessings.

Without true devotion even great erudition will not prevent doubts about the teacher from arising. Without true devotion we may fall into the error of viewing the guru's deeds in a biased way, thus cultivating a perverse attitude toward him. In the end, we may become even more deeply obscured than when we first met the teacher. But, if we cultivate heartfelt devotion, then simply through this intense fervor we will be liberated.

We may not feel such devotion from the very moment we meet the teacher; so, as a means of engendering greater and greater devotion, we practice a guru yoga sādhana, in which we perceive the teacher as inseparable from a perfect form such as Guru Padmasambhava, also known as Guru Rinpoche, the Precious Guru. In the beginning, we may have to generate a kind of artificial devotion, a mental construct. At this point, we would meditate that our guru is indissociable from Guru Rinpoche.

Who, we may ask, is Guru Rinpoche? In the dharmakāya, the absolute level, he is Buddha Öpame (Skt. Amitābha). In the sambhogakāya, the level of "divine enjoyment," he is Chenrezik (Skt. Avalokiteśvara). In the *nirmāṇakāya*, the level of manifestation, he is the Lotus-Born Guru Pema Jungne (Skt. Padmākara), who appeared in this degenerate age when sentient beings, obscured by the afflictions of gross negative emotions and erroneous views, are disinclined to practice the sublime dharma. In this dark age, beings are afflicted with the three calamities of sickness, famine, and warfare. It is in such an age that Guru Padmasambhava manifested as the embodiment of all the buddhas. He came to Tibet in the form of an Indian *siddha* and disclosed all the instructions to his twenty-five disciples, to the eighty siddhas of Yerpa, and to many others, all of whom eventually achieved full realization.

We too, in these days, through the immense kindness of Guru Rinpoche, are able to practice the teachings of the Secret Mantrayāna vehicle. In order to generate the perception of our teacher as being one with the Lotus-Born Guru, we should generate, from the core of our heart, the following thought: "My guru is identical with Guru Rinpoche. He has the same realization and he is able to display all the miracles and enlightened qualities that Guru Rinpoche manifested in his life."

Initially, this thought is generated in an artificial way

by repeating it over and over again; however, with intense conviction, a genuine and effortless devotion will take birth in us. In the same way that the gilding of a buddha image makes it even more resplendent, the meditation upon our teacher as inseparable from Guru Padmasambhava will make it that much easier for us to receive blessings and engender deep devotion.

Throughout the practice of guru yoga, the mere recitation of the verses is insufficient, since the main point is the generation of devotion. To accomplish this, during meditation the mind should not wander, with restless thoughts going here and there; the body should remain in the seven-point posture; the mantra recitation should not merely be mouthed, but rather spoken with faith aroused from the depths of our hearts, from the very marrow of our bones, and with the conviction that our guru is truly Guru Rinpoche himself.

In general, the performance of any action with the body, speech, and mind in unison will generate a greater result. If, for example, we perform the offering of prostrations by putting the body through a series of mechanical movements while speech engages in conversations and the mind makes plans for the future or dallies with a thousand thoughts of the past, then the prostrations will be of little benefit.

With the body we should do prostrations carefully; with the speech we should recite the refuge prayer clearly without interspersing it with ordinary words; and with the mind we should concentrate fully on the practice with heartfelt devotion. We should remember that when performing a prostration, placing the hands at the three centers of forehead, throat, and heart, we pay homage to the body, speech, and mind of all the buddhas. We thus receive the corresponding blessings, which purify the three poisons and all negativity of our body, speech, and mind.

When someone engages in a worldly undertaking, in order to succeed he will coordinate his body, speech, and mind in a harmonious and consistent way. He will be so concerned about the outcome that he will think about it day and night. Similarly, if we are able to identify our goals precisely and make ceaseless efforts toward these ends, uniting the activities of body, speech, and mind, there is no doubt that we will succeed swiftly. Otherwise, if we practice in a hypocritical way, like a person who is performing in the presence of a king or dignitary, pretending to be very diligent with the body while the mind entertains no genuine interest, there will not be much progress. It would then be a mere exercise that brings no result and leads to nothing. The drawing of a butter lamp on a wall looks like a butter lamp, but does not dispel darkness.

This is why we should coordinate and unify the body, speech, and mind when practicing. Among these three, the mind is the most important, as the body and speech will follow wherever the mind leads. Mind therefore should not be allowed to wander.

There are three main parts to the actual practice of guru yoga. First, there is the visualization of the object of meditation and the invitation to the *jñānasattva* to descend. Next is the prayer in seven branches. Finally, there is the fervent supplication to the guru and the receiving of the four empowerments.

The Visualization

The Place as a Buddha-Field

In any visualization practice we should think that everything has been perfect from the very beginning, that what we visualize is not an intellectual product but primordially true. This means that we perceive the natural perfection of the environment as a buddha-field and the beings therein as celestial beings, ḍākas, and ḍākinīs. With intense devotion, we perceive our teacher as inseparable from Guru Padmasambhava. If we maintain constant devotion, it is certain that Guru Rinpoche will always be near us, like our shadow. In order to support and vivify such devotion, we recite the verses of this guru yoga.

The first verse opens with "*Emaho,*" an expression of wonder, and continues with the words: "The self-appearing, naturally present, perfectly pure, infinite buddha-field. . . ." This refers to Guru Rinpoche's paradise, the Glorious Copper-Colored Mountain, Sangdopalri, where beings are naturally free from the poisonous emotions, naturally inclined to practice the dharma, and where one can see Guru Rinpoche face to face. This is what is called a "pure buddha-field." In contrast to this, we have this ordinary place where the beings are filled with strong poisons, such as craving, anger, pride, jealousy, and miserliness, where they do not behave in accordance with the dharma, and where they are completely distracted by aims limited to this lifetime. This is what is called an "impure field."

If we visualize the place around us as an impure field, it will not help us. But if we visualize it as a pure buddha-field, it will become so; or, to be more exact, we will come to realize its natural purity. Thus, we should visualize the place as a self-appearing buddha-field encompassing the whole of manifested reality. In the present guru yoga, this perfectly arranged buddha-field is the Glorious Copper-Colored Mountain, Sangdopalri, the paradise of Guru Rinpoche.

Such a buddha-field is composed not of ordinary earth and rock, but of precious jewels. There are wish-fulfilling trees as well as a lake of nectarlike water that possesses the eight qualities[27] and that confers immortality. Even the wild animals living there behave in harmony with the dharma. The calls of the birds carry the sound of dharma, and all natural sounds of water, wind, fire, and forests reverberate as mantras. The sky is filled with rainbows and *vidyādhara*s, ḍakas, and ḍākinīs, numberless as dust particles in the sun rays. Celestial music, *vajra* songs, and melodious tunes of mantras resound, bringing inexpressible bliss to the mind. The beings are not divided into those whom we see as friends and those whom we see as enemies, but all have the nature and appearance of ḍākas and ḍākinīs. All are companions on the path, behaving in accordance with the dharma. In this buddha-field we perceive beings as free from the poisons of jealousy, pride, and aggression, and, without judging some to be superior and others inferior, we generate the same loving-kindness and equanimity to all.

If we hold in our minds this visualized buddha-field, our manner of perceiving things will gradually change. We will perceive all as pure and will be able to see the paradise of the Glorious Copper-Colored Mountain everywhere. If, for instance, we see frescoes depicting the life of Lord Buddha on the walls of a temple, our devotion increases. If the walls were simply left plain white, they would inspire nothing. To keep visualizing a place as a paradise works in a similar way.

In brief, we should perceive all the forms we see as being the display of Guru Rinpoche's body, all the sounds we hear as mantra, the voice of Guru Rinpoche, and whatever thoughts or recollections that occur in our minds as the display of the perfect wisdom of Guru Rinpoche's mind. We should not think that this is a mental fabrication, but that things have naturally been this way since the very beginning. This pure state is something that naturally exists, but of which we are not aware. Through the practice of guru yoga we will gradually come to recognize the true nature of phenomena. The purpose of the meditation is thus to uncloud our mistaken perception of things and to realize, instead, the innate purity of all phenomena.

Ourselves as Vajrayoginī

In the same way, we must visualize ourselves as someone extraordinary, here as Vajrayoginī, the mother, or source, of all the buddhas. She has one face, two arms, and two legs. She is brilliant red, bright and transparent, not made of gross material elements like flesh, blood, and bones, but instead clear as though made of light. All the details of her appearance, down to her ornaments and the black and white of her eyes, are perceived in very fine and precise detail. She has three eyes, which gaze skyward with great devotion toward Guru Rinpoche, filled with the joy of meeting the guru. Her lips are slightly parted, revealing her teeth, thus adding a somewhat wrathful aspect to her otherwise peaceful expression. She gazes with one-pointed mind toward Guru Rinpoche, just as a man and woman who feel great affection gaze upon each other. She is standing in a dancing posture with her right leg slightly bent, her right heel raised off the ground as if ready to step forward, and her left foot on the ground. She stands upon a lotus, a sun, a moon, and a corpse. In her right hand she wields a curved knife, which is raised toward the sky, symbolizing cutting through ego and the three poisons of attachment, anger, and ignorance. In her left hand she holds a skull cup filled with *amṛita*, the nectar of deathlessness. In the crook of her left arm rests the *khaṭvāṅga*, or trident, which symbolizes Guru Rinpoche in a hidden form. She is adorned with the eight bone ornaments set with jewels: diadem, earrings, three kinds of necklaces, bracelets, anklets, and belt, symbolizing the transmutation of the eight consciousnesses[28] into wisdom. She also wears the five silk scarves symbolizing the five wisdoms. In form, she is Vajrayoginī, but in nature she is Yeshe Tsogyal.

The visualization of ourselves as Yeshe Tsogyal is particularly important and profound. She was both Guru Rinpoche's consort and his chief disciple. He had a deep loving-kindness and a great tenderness toward her, as well as confidence in her ability to understand and implement his teachings. Thus, if we visualize ourselves as Yeshe Tsogyal, with Guru Rinpoche dwelling upon the crown of our head, naturally our devotion will be strongly enhanced and the stream of blessings will flow more swiftly into us.

Who, actually, was Yeshe Tsogyal? She never entertained any wrong views or doubts about Guru Rinpoche even for a single instant and always perceived him as the Buddha in person. Because of her total and unshakable devotion she was a perfect vessel for all of Guru Rinpoche's precious instructions. Thus she was able to practice flawlessly and to attain perfect realization. Ultimately, there was not the slightest difference between her realization and that of Guru Rinpoche.

Visualizing ourselves as Yeshe Tsogyal creates an auspicious connection through which we can receive, like Yeshe Tsogyal, all the blessings and teachings of Guru Rinpoche, and which will enable us to practice them and to attain enlightenment. She is perceived as being the mother of all the buddhas and, just as in any family where the children have great affection for their mother, we should think that all the buddhas have great love and affection for us.

Guru Rinpoche above Our Head

Above the crown of our head, upon a lotus of one hundred thousand petals, are two disks of sun and moon. The sun disk represents the skillful means of compassion, while the moon disk represents the wisdom of realizing emptiness. Both disks are full and flat, one floating slightly above the other, and both are floating slightly above the lotus. Upon these is seated our guru in the form of Guru Rinpoche, in whom all objects of refuge are one. In outward aspect he is the union of the three jewels: Buddha, dharma, and *saṅgha*. In inner aspect he is the union of the three roots: *lama, yidam,* and ḍākinī. In secret aspect he is the union of the three kāyas: dharmakāya, sambhogakāya and nirmāṇakāya.[29] In nature he is our kind root teacher who, in this present life, is granting us all the instructions.

In appearance he is the Lake-Born One, Guru Padmasambhava, who is both the union and essence of all the buddhas of the past, present, and future, manifesting here in nirmāṇakāya form. His body has the indestructible nature of a vajra, or diamond. To indicate his attainment of immortality, he has the countenance of an eight-year-old child resplendent with youth. His complexion is white, tinged slightly with red, glowing with health.

He is dressed in the nine robes, which signify his mastery of the nine *yānas*. These include a garment of white beneath a blue robe and the three monastic robes. Over these he wears a brocade cape. The three monastic robes indicate his mastery of the teachings of the Hīnayāna; the blue garment indicates his mastery of the teachings of the Mahāyāna, the path of the bodhisattvas; and the brocade cape indicates his mastery of the secret teachings of the Vajrayāna, the secret mantra vehicle.

He has one face, two arms, and two legs. His eyes are wide open, gazing straight into the sky, indicating that he is always aware of the absolute nature. There is a slight frown or crease of the forehead between the eyebrows, although his mouth is set in a smile; thus he unites in himself both peaceful and wrathful aspects. He is seated in the posture called "royal ease," his right leg slightly extended and his left leg drawn up into a sitting posture. Just as no one would disobey the command of a king, there is no one in the three worlds of saṃsāra who would disobey the command of Guru Rinpoche, the king of absolute wisdom.

In his right hand he holds a five-pronged golden vajra, here symbolizing the fruition of all the qualities of the first of the four initiations, the vase initiation. In many of his representations Guru Rinpoche wields this golden vajra in a pointed-finger gesture at the level of his heart center. Here, however, in this decadent age when the victory banner is hoisted by the dark forces of negativity, Guru Rinpoche raises his all-subduing vajra toward the sky. This particular gesture, or *mudrā*, is found elsewhere in the Longchen Nyingthig, in the sādhana called Rigdzin Düpa, and is known as Nangsi Zilnön, or "Conquering Appearance and Existence."

His left hand, which rests in the mudrā of equanimity, holds a nectar-filled skull cup, which has all the perfect qualities and characteristics. This skull cup symbolizes the fruition of the second or secret initiation. The skull cup is surmounted by the vase of immortality, indicating that Guru Rinpoche has attained the level of the vidyādhara of immortality, or "one who holds the knowledge of immortality." The vase is adorned at its top with branches of the wish-fulfilling tree.

Although Guru Rinpoche can be represented wearing various kinds of hats or crowns, in this case he wears the five-petaled lotus crown. These five petals symbolize the five buddha families, and, since Guru Rinpoche is an emanation of the buddha of the *padma* family, Amitābha, the crown is in the form of a lotus. The lotus crown also indicates that, like a lotus rising free and unstained above the mud below, Guru Rinpoche manifested miraculously, unstained by the obscuring process of an ordinary birth. At the top of the hat are a sun and a moon, symbolizing means and wisdom, surmounted by a white vulture feather symbolizing the realization of the ultimate view, the Great Perfection.

In the crook of his left arm rests the khaṭvāṅga, or trident, symbolizing the fruition of the third or wisdom initiation. The khaṭvāṅga is also a hidden form of the ḍākinīs Yeshe Tsogyal and Mandāravā, the chief consorts of Guru Rinpoche, who themselves represent bliss and emptiness. The three prongs symbolize the void nature of all appearance, its expression as pure luminosity, and compassion, which is all-encompassing. From each of the prongs hang three rings, symbolizing together the nine vehicles. Below the prongs, from the top, are a dry skull, a decaying head, and a freshly severed head, symbolizing the three times and the three kāyas. Below these are a vase of long life, a pair of crossed vajras, and a *ḍamaru*, or skull drum, adorned with silk scarves, whose five colors symbolize the five wisdoms.

Guru Rinpoche sits in space filled with intermingled rays of rainbow light and constellated with dots and circles of the five colors. Boundless and infinite rays of light stream from his body to all the ten directions. From this streaming light he can emanate, according to his wish, all the buddha-fields of the ten directions, as well as all the buddhas and bodhisattvas and all the deities of the three roots. All of these are emanations of his wisdom heart. He can in the same way gather them back into his body, thereby demonstrating that they are all one with him.

There are three main ways of visualizing Guru Rinpoche. The first is visualizing Guru Rinpoche alone as the "one jewel that embodies all"; the second is visualizing Guru Rinpoche with all the precious teachers arrayed in tiers one below the other, from the primordial Buddha Samantabhadra down to Guru Rinpoche himself. Here we will visualize according to a third method, called the "great gathering." In this practice we visualize Guru Rinpoche at the center of a cloudlike gathering of gurus and deities and surrounded by the assembly of all his heart disciples. These disciples are actually emanations of his body, speech, mind, qualities, and action, and as each of these aspects is further subdivided according to the same five categories, there are twenty-five heart disciples in all. These include Vairocana, Namkhe Nyingpo, King Trisong Detsen, Khandro Yeshe Tsogyal, Nanam Dorje Dudjom, and so forth. Also in the crowd of great beings around Guru Rinpoche are the eight Vidyādharas of India, holders of the eight transmissions. These include Mañjuśrīmitra, holder of the transmission of the body aspect of the yidam, the wrathful Mañjuśrī;

Nāgārjuna, holder of the transmission of the speech aspect, Hayagrīva; and Hūṃchenkāra, holder of the mind aspect, Yangdak Heruka.

Other members of this vast assembly are the eighty-four mahāsiddhas of India and all the accomplished sages and yogis of the various schools and lineages that flourished in Tibet, such as the Nyingma, Sakya, Kagyu, Shangpa Kagyu, Jor-druk, Urgyen Nyengyu, Zhi-che, Kadam, and Geluk.[30] They thus form an immense retinue around Guru Rinpoche, consisting of all those to whom we have devotion. We meditate that all these great teachers are above our head, with the thought that in our past lives we have received instruction from each of them. In this way we should generate great gratitude and great devotion, thinking ourselves to be like Shönnu Lobsang, the "Intelligent Young One," who attended over one hundred fifty teachers to reach enlightenment.

Surrounding these, we visualize all the *yidams* of the four sections of the tantras, the ḍākinīs and protectors of the father and mother lineages, the buddhas, bodhisattvas, arhats, and pratyekabuddhas. Just as the peaks of lofty mountains are encircled by great clouds, so is Guru Rinpoche surrounded by all of these beings.

In order to correct our ordinary impure perception of phenomena, we should not visualize them with gross material bodies of flesh, bone, and blood, but rather as bodies of light—very clear and transparent, with a vivid rainbowlike appearance. They appear clearly, yet are empty of substance, like the reflection of the moon in water. At the same time, we should not feel that they are inert, lifeless displays of rainbow light, but that they are completely filled with wisdom, loving-kindness, and the ability to benefit beings.

Although we visualize Guru Rinpoche as a main figure

surrounded by an infinite retinue, there is in actuality no distinction or separation between them: all deities and beings in the visualization are emanations of Guru Rinpoche himself. Since they are the display of his mind and are thus by nature identical with him, their wisdom and compassion are equal to his own.

It is said that through strong aspiration and fervor anything can be accomplished. Similarly, if we think without the slightest doubt that Guru Rinpoche is truly present above our head, his blessings will flow down to us without interruption. We must not think that he is possibly there, that he might be there at some future time, or that the Guru Rinpoche visualized above our head is no more than a mental construct or a substitute slightly inferior to the actual Guru Rinpoche who dwells on the distant Copper-Colored Mountain. We should be absolutely confident that he is present with all of his wisdom and compassion, and we should think that it is only due to our obscurations that we cannot readily perceive him. Furthermore, we should not think that Guru Rinpoche dwells in so distant a place as to be unaware of us or of our supplications to him, or that in caring for so many sentient beings he could not possibly notice us or remember us. Guru Rinpoche has complete wisdom, loving-kindness, and ability. We must realize that even a prayer to Guru Rinpoche, the recitation of a single Vajra Guru mantra calling upon him, or even the raising of a single hand toward our heart in a gesture of devotion toward him or simply remembering him with clear faith, will be perceived by him, for he has full knowledge of our devotion. As it is said, "The Buddha dwells in front of whosoever has faith in him."

Even if, at the same instant, an infinite number of sentient beings are praying to him, he will know precisely how each is praying, precisely who is suffering, and precisely who is happy. He will know on which level each being is, and he will know which prayer each makes and whether or not it comes from the depth of the heart. He will know all these things with great clarity, with the vividness of an image in a mirror. Guru Rinpoche himself said: "I stand before the door of whoever has devotion." He will always accompany us, as close as our own shadow. If we have devotion, it is promised that all the buddhas of the three times will remain with us.

This is the promise of Guru Rinpoche, who, as the emanation of the body, speech, and mind of all the buddhas, manifested especially to meet the needs of the beings of this decadent age. His prayers and compassion have great efficacy in the alleviation of the suffering of the epidemics, famines, and wars that beset such an age. Now, when all beings are afflicted with gross poisons, when nothing remains but residues of the good qualities of former times, and when the negative influences of irreligious vow-breakers are rampant, we must pray especially to Guru Rinpoche so that he will subdue all negative forces and pacify all torments.

We must also have firm faith that our own teacher, whom we can meet face to face in this life and from whom we can hear the pith instructions directly, is identical with Guru Rinpoche. Praying to our own guru will bring us blessings even more swiftly. When rain falls upon a roof, the drainpipe collects all the water. In the same way, if we pray to our own teacher as inseparable from Guru Rinpoche, we will be able to gather all blessings.

Guru Rinpoche, as the embodiment of all the buddhas of the three times, displays many aspects. No matter which of his aspects is the object of our supplications, our aspirations will be fulfilled. In the prayer known as the "Spontaneous Fulfillment of All Aspirations," if we are stricken by illness or if our life is endangered, we supplicate Guru Rinpoche in his aspect as Amitāyus, the Buddha of Infinite Life. If we are destitute and deprived of everything, we supplicate him in his aspect as the Deity of Prosperity. If we are threatened by the natural environment, we supplicate him in his aspect as Master of the Elements. If attacked by wild animals or other assailants, we supplicate him as the Invincible Hero. If afflicted by disease, we supplicate him as the Medicine Buddha of Urgyen. If death comes upon us without warning, we supplicate him in his aspect as the Buddha Amitābha, "Infinite Light." If we are tormented by fears of the *bardo*, we supplicate him in his aspect as the One Who Knows the Three Times. Guru Rinpoche's nature as union of all the buddhas makes possible this vast array of manifestations. Ultimately, if we pray to Guru Rinpoche as the one essence of all the buddhas, we will attain the supreme siddhi of the realization of our own inherent wisdom-nature. Pray in this way with one-pointed concentration and with full confidence, and there is not the slightest doubt that the supplications will be answered. This is why in this prayer Guru Rinpoche says as many as thirteen times: "Pray with an undivided mind free of doubts."

The Invitation of the Wisdom Deity

The next step in the sādhana is the invitation to Guru Rinpoche to come from his buddha-field and bless us. Why do we need to invite him if we are confident that he is actually present above our head? As beginners, we are not completely free of the thought that Guru Rinpoche continues to dwell far away in the celestial buddha-field of the Glorious Copper-Colored Mountain. In order to eliminate this doubt, we invite him to come from his buddha-field. Believing that he actually does come and that he dissolves into the Guru Rinpoche that we visualize dwelling above the crown of our head, our visualization is empowered much in the same way a statue is filled with sacred relics or an inert body is endowed with a mind. We should then think that Guru Rinpoche is truly abiding with us, both in aspect and in essence, and through this belief our devotion and fervor will greatly increase.

To generate and sustain our devotion and to invite Guru Rinpoche, we use the prayer in seven lines known as the "Seven Diamond Verses." There are many prayers of varying lengths that invoke Guru Rinpoche, from the extensive "Prayer in Seven Chapters" to the moderately long prayer to Guru Rinpoche that "Removes All Obstacles Along the Path," and the prayer for the "Spontaneous Fulfillment of All Aspirations." The most condensed and essential prayer, however, is the "Seven Diamond Verses," also known as the "Seven-Line Prayer."

This is a prayer of immense power. For instance, Guru Rinpoche, having resolved out of compassion to manifest in our world, emerged from the heart of Amitābha in the form of a red letter HRĪḤ, which, amid boundless rays of light, descended and came to rest on a red lotus blossom in the center of Dhanakośa Lake in northwest Oḍḍiyāṇa. Then, in an instant, the letter HRĪḤ transformed into an eight-year-old boy—Guru Rinpoche, the Lotus-Born. He did all this specifically in response to the fervent recitation of the "Seven Diamond Verses," by means of which the ḍākas and ḍākinīs entreated him to appear in this universe.

In another instance, during a time when Guru Rinpoche was dwelling in India, the Land of the Noble One,[31] a great debate was held between the Buddhist and *tīrthika*[32] *paṇḍitas* who were in residence at Dorje Den (Skt. Vajrāsana, the "Diamond Throne" of India, present-day Bodhgayā). As the debate progressed, it seemed as though the Buddhists were going to lose the contest. One night many of them had a visionary dream in which a ḍākinī in the form of an old woman appeared and predicted their imminent defeat. She explained that their only hope for victory lay in receiving the aid of her elder brother, who was at that moment performing yogic practices in one of the great cemeteries of India. His name was Dorje Thötrengtsal, "Vajra Strength of the Skull Garland." She said that were they to make strong entreaties to him, he would without question come and vanquish the heretic paṇḍitas. The Buddhist scholars feared that the distances were too great for Dorje Thötrengtsal to be able to arrive in time to save the debate; they felt that only a miracle would be able to bring him soon enough. The ḍākinī reassured them, explaining that for Guru Rinpoche time and distance posed no hindrance. She urged the paṇḍitas to make a great offering on the roof of their temple and to invite Guru Rinpoche through the fervent invocation of the "Seven Diamond Verses." She promised that if they proceeded in this manner, Guru Rinpoche would come.

The next day, discovering that many of their number had had the same dream, they followed the instructions of the ḍākinī. Just as she had promised, Guru Rinpoche appeared in the sky and then sat down in their midst as the chief scholar, ready to dispute with the heretic teachers. In the course of the debate, he destroyed their arguments, using both his mastery of the scriptures and his wisdom. The tīrthikas, in desperation, fell back upon their skills in magic to put a curse upon the Buddhist scholars. Guru Rinpoche then went to the Cool Forest charnel ground, where the Lion-Headed Ḍākinī, Senge Dongma, appeared to him and told him to meditate upon her and recite her mantra for seven days, after which Guru Rinpoche, bringing down thunder and lightning upon the heretics, utterly vanquished them. After this the heretics entered the Buddhist path.

The "Seven-Line Prayer" carries very great blessings. Among all the *terma*s, or rediscovered spiritual treasures, found in ancient or recent times that address Guru Rinpoche, there is not a single one in which the "Seven-Line Prayer" is not found. As Guru Rinpoche said: "When a disciple calls upon me with devotion and the yearning song of the 'Seven-Line Prayer,' I shall come at once from Sangdopalri, like a mother who cannot resist the call of her child."

The prayer begins with the letter HŪNG, which is the seed syllable of the heart-wisdom of all the buddhas. It continues, saying, "*Urgyen yul gyi nup chang tsam,*" which means, "At the northwest border of the land of Oḍḍiyāṇa." In this land there are four lakes, one in each of the four directions. It is in the lake situated in the northwest corner, known as Dhanakośa, that Guru Rinpoche manifested in this world. In Sanskrit, *dhana* means "wealth," and *kośa* means "treasury."

The second line, "*Pema gesar dong po la,*" means "On the pistil of a lotus blossom." In Dhanakośa Lake there are innumerable lotuses of the five colors. Since Guru Rinpoche belongs to the speech or lotus family, the family of Amitābha, whose color is red, he manifested in the middle of the lake upon the pistil of a red lotus.

The third line, "*Yam tsen chok kyi ngo drup nye,*" means "The marvelous one who has attained the supreme accomplishment." Guru Rinpoche was not born from causes and conditions or from the seeds of a mother and father, but, as we have said, arose suddenly from the center of a red lotus in the form of the seed syllable HRĪḤ, as a manifestation of pure awareness from the heart of Amitābha. The HRĪḤ then melted into light, transforming into the aspect of an ever-youthful eight-year-old child with radiant countenance and the thirty-two major and eighty minor marks of a buddha. He thus appeared in our universe amid rainbows, a rain of flowers thrown by all the buddhas of the ten directions, celestial music, and melodious songs of praise sung by the countless ḍākas and ḍākinīs who filled the sky.

The fourth line, "*Pema Jungne shey su drak,*" means "Renowned as the Lotus-Born." Guru Rinpoche, the ultimate and undeceiving object of refuge, is renowned throughout the infinity of buddha-fields as the Guru Born from the Lotus.

The fifth line, "*Khor du khandro mang po kor,*" means "Surrounded by a retinue of many ḍākinīs." Wherever Guru Rinpoche manifests, he unfolds and expounds the teachings of the secret Mantrayāna or Vajrayāna. Since the ḍākinīs are those who both hear and hold these teachings, Guru Rinpoche is always surrounded by a gathering of ḍākinīs.

In the sixth line, "*Kye kyi jesu da drup kyi,*" we pray, "Following in your footsteps, I myself will become accomplished." At present, owing to our ignorance, we are wandering helplessly among the delusions and sufferings of saṃsāra; the only way out of this situation is to receive the profound instructions of the secret Mantrayāna and put them into practice. Thus, in order to clear away our ignorance, we invite Guru Rinpoche with our supplications to come and give us the blessings, empowerments, and instructions we need to enable us to follow him on the path and accomplish, as he has, the supreme realization. Obscured by karma and the force of negative emotions and submerged in ignorance, we are at this moment drowning in the ocean of suffering. If we fail to rely on an extraordinary being like Guru Rinpoche who is himself free from this ocean, then there is no way for us to be delivered from this misery and confusion.

The seventh line is "*Chin gyi lop chir shek su sol,*" or "Please come and bless me." When, through our entreaties, Guru Rinpoche comes and bestows upon us the blessings of his body, speech, and mind, we are enabled to achieve realization. As the gilding of a statue makes it even more beautiful and precious, so our own body, speech, and mind, when blessed by the body, speech, and mind of Guru Rinpoche, become better able to achieve the supreme accomplishment.

The prayer closes with the mantra "*Guru pema siddhi hung.*" *Guru* is a Sanskrit word that literally means "heavy." It was translated into Tibetan as *lama,* which literally means "unsurpassable." "Heavy" shows that the guru is heavy with good qualities and that to transgress his instructions will bring heavy consequences. Guru Rinpoche is the quintessence, the complete union, of all the wisdom, loving-kindness, and abilities of the buddhas of the three times. Thus, as he is full of innumerable enlightened qualities, we call him "guru," heavy. The Sanskrit word *padma* (used also in Tibetan and pronounced *pema*) means "lotus." It refers to Padmasambhava's name. As an emanation of the heart of the Buddha Amitābha, Guru Rinpoche belongs to the lotus or speech family of buddhas and is himself a vidyādhara or awareness-holder of this buddha family; also, he was born in the heart of a lotus. The Sanskrit *siddhi* or Tibetan *ngödrup* can be understood in English as "true accomplishment." HŪNG is the seed syllable of the mind of all the buddhas, and, as all the buddhas are embodied in him, it is especially the seed syllable of Guru Rinpoche. Thus, when at the end of the prayer we say "SIDDHI HŪNG," we are asking him to grant us all the accomplishments, both common and supreme.

If we recite this prayer with deep devotion again and again, there is no doubt that we will receive the blessings. We should develop unshakable confidence that, in answer to our invocation and invitation, Guru Rinpoche will actually come to us from the paradise of the Glorious Copper-Colored Mountain.

Having visualized ourselves as Vajrayoginī, we should think that another Vajrayoginī, identical to ourselves, approaches us from the sky. Upon her head, just as upon our own head, is Guru Rinpoche, surrounded by the eight vidyādharas of India, his twenty-five Tibetan heart-disciples, and a cloudlike retinue of ḍākas, ḍākinīs, lamas, yidams, protectors, and so forth. Vajrayoginī, Guru Rinpoche, and the rest descend upon us and dissolve into us: Vajrayoginī dissolves into Vajrayoginī, Guru Rinpoche into Guru Rinpoche, and the vast retinue into the vast retinue. Looking up at him with complete devotion, we should believe without the slightest doubt that Guru Rinpoche himself is there upon our heads, and that he will bestow his blessings on us.

So, having visualized one Guru Rinpoche above our heads, we have invited another to come and dissolve into the first one: this first Guru Rinpoche is called the *samayasattva* and the Guru Rinpoche who comes to us from his buddha-field is called the jñānasattva. When the jñānasattva melts into the samayasattva, it is as if milk has been poured into water; the two blend so intimately that it is impossible to distinguish between them, and the water becomes enriched and more delicious than before. In the same way, when we invite Guru Rinpoche to dissolve into the one we have visualized above our head, we should think that his blessing, compassion, and wisdom are even more intensely present and immense.

The Seven Branches

In order to receive the blessings of Guru Rinpoche, we should also complete the accumulations of merit and wisdom. For this the easiest and most essential method is the one in seven branches. According to ordinary custom, when greeting an important person we offer him some token of our respect, some form of deference such as a bow, a comfortable place to sit, and then some delicious things to eat and drink. Similarly, but on a loftier plane, when we invite the Lotus-Born Guru from his buddha-field, we make offerings to him. In general, there is inconceivably great merit in making offerings to the buddhas. It is said, however, that to offer just a single drop of oil to a single pore of the body of the guru has more merits and benefits than to make infinite offerings to all the buddhas. In particular, if we make offerings, prostrations, or the confession of faults in front of the guru, the merit and benefits will be greatly enhanced and the purification of our obscurations and defilements swifter.

Prostration

The first of the seven branches is prostration, the antidote to pride. Visualizing ourselves as Vajrayoginī, we now emanate a second Vajrayoginī, who, with Guru Rinpoche dwelling above the crown of her head, stands before us. From ourselves we then emanate bodies as numerous as the particles of dust in the universe. We and all our emanations, joined by all the beings of the universe, begin to offer prostrations to Guru Rinpoche and chant the refuge prayer in unison.

To make prostrations, we should begin by standing in a well-balanced position. We join the palms of our hands together, cupping them slightly to form the shape of a lotus bud ready to bloom, symbolizing the generation of *bodhicitta*. We next place our joined hands at the level of the forehead, thinking, "I pay homage to the body aspect of all the buddhas." Here we are purifying all the obscurations and negative actions of the body. We then bring our joined hands to the level of the throat, thinking, "I pay homage to the speech aspect of all the buddhas." Here, all our obscurations and defilements connected with speech are purified. Bringing our joined hands to the level of the heart, we think, "I pay homage to the mind aspect of all the buddhas." Here, all our obscurations and negative emotions are purified. Through this series of gestures and thoughts, we receive the blessings of the body, speech, and mind of all the buddhas.

When we make the prostration, touching the ground at five points—with our forehead, two hands, and two knees—we should think that in this way we pay homage to the five buddha families, and in this way we transform the five poisons into the five wisdoms.

The full prostration, known as the prostration of devotion, done by stretching out flat on the ground with arms and legs fully extended, brings even greater benefits and a swifter purification. As we rise from this full prostration, our hands sliding back along the ground, we should think that we are taking up into ourselves the suffering of all beings.

We use our body to make physical prostrations, our speech to recite the prayer of the seven branches, and our mind to visualize Guru Rinpoche in front of us surrounded by his cloudlike retinue. We should practice mindfulness with respect to each of these aspects, striving to maintain clarity and precision in the visualization, awareness of the meaning of the recitation, and attention to the body so that it performs with balance, propriety, poise, and discipline.

There are three levels to the prostration practice. At the highest level we recognize the view of the absolute nature, the essence of buddhahood. This recognition is itself the most profound and reverent prostration. At the intermediate level we blend our meditation with the act of prostration as we visualize an infinity of beings and emanations of ourselves making prostrations together. At the ordinary level we perform the prostration with mindfulness and faith.

It is said that in the performance of a single prostration there is enough merit to ensure as many births in the form of a universal monarch as there are particles of dust beneath our outstretched body. This is because genuine humility is the open door to all greatness of being, while pride, the fortress of the ego, completely prevents the blessings of the buddhas from entering us, thus forestalling any progress on the path.

Offering

The second of the seven branches, offering, the antidote to greed and miserliness, has two aspects: the outer or material offerings and the inner or mental offerings. Upon the altar we place water bowls, flowers, incense, lamps, scented water, food, and an offering symbolic of music. These are the seven traditional material offerings. Through our power of concentration we can offer the vast display of all phenomena, referred to as the "mudrā of existence." This means that we make an offering of the entire universe, not in an ordinary but in a glorified form. For example, mountains, ordinarily splendid, are here made entirely of gold, silver, coral, jewels, and all kinds of precious substances; forests are lush with wish-fulfilling trees; and lakes and rivers are filled with amṛita, the nectar of immortality. We offer not only these things, but also all we see around us that is pleasing or beautiful, such as gardens and parks, flowers, birds, and animals, and even the magnificence of large cities with all their richness and variety. All of this we offer to Guru Rinpoche and his retinue of buddhas and bodhisattvas, thereby accumulating great merit.

The most extraordinary and effective way of making such offering is the Cloudlike Offering of Samantabhadra: visualizing ourselves as the bodhisattva Samantabhadra, we emanate from our heart thousands of brilliant rays of light, each of which carries vast offerings to the buddhas of the ten directions. On the very tip of each of these rays we generate an emanation of ourselves as Samantabhadra, from whose heart shine thousands of rays of light bearing even vaster offerings. On the tip of each of these rays is again Samantabhadra, and again light rays and offerings, and so on, until all the great immensity of space is completely filled with offerings beyond measure.

Additionally, we should offer from the very depths of our heart whatever in the world we cherish most, such as our own body, our children, our spouse, our property, and so forth. We should make as many offerings, both mental and material, as we can, such as thousands, tens of thousands, or hundreds of thousands of butter lamps. In this way, we will progress rapidly on the path.

Confession

The third branch is confession. While remaining aware of the expanse of the luminous dharmakāya, or absolute state, we confess all the negative actions of body, speech, and mind that hinder our progress toward enlightenment.

Since beginningless time we have been taking rebirth in the ocean of saṃsāra. Though a buddha in his omniscience knows each of the lives we have lived, even were he to speak for an entire kalpa he would be unable to describe all of them. Throughout each of these innumerable lives, we have been accumulating the imprints of negative actions. Of the body, these include killing, taking what is not given, and sexual misconduct. Of speech, they include the telling of lies, slandering others, idle gossip, and piercing the heart of another with harsh words. Of the mind, they include envy, the wish to harm others, and adherence to false views. Other negative actions of the three doors involve transgressions of the *prātimokṣa* vows, the bodhisattva vows, and the *samaya*s of secret Mantrayāna.[33] What we call nonvirtue, or negative action, is not something visible, like paint, but is rather more akin to a seed planted in the ground of our consciousness or a letter of debt bound to come to maturation. All of our actions, whether white or black, will inescapably come to fruition. It is the very inevitability or certainty of this fruition that makes the confession and purification of our negative actions imperative. We should never think, for instance, that a very small negative action, like saying a bad word to someone, will have no consequences; the effect of any action, no matter how small, will never simply vanish into thin air, but will in its time bear fruit.

Although our negative actions may not ripen during

the course of this lifetime, they will definitely do so at the time of our death, much in the same way that the shadow of a bird, invisible while the bird is aloft, appears suddenly the moment the bird alights on the ground. After death, when our consciousness is wandering in the bardo,[34] the force of our negative actions will impel us into the terrible suffering of the rebirth in the lower realms. At present we have the opportunity to purify these negative actions and their effects through the practice of confession.

It is said that the only good quality of negative action is that it can be purified. In fact, there is no negative action so grievous that it cannot be purified.

We can begin to purify this negativity by using and relying upon four strengths. The first of these is the *strength of support.* In our effort to repair the damage caused by our negative actions, we need an appropriate object as support for our confession. In this instance, it is Guru Rinpoche. We visualize him in front of ourselves and offer our confession to him.

The second is the *strength of remorse.* This is sincere regret for our actions and sorrow at having committed them. This regret arises when we think, "How dismaying that through the power of all the negative actions I have repeatedly committed throughout the course of my countless past lives, I am now bound to be reborn among the animals, hungry ghosts, or hell beings. It is these negative actions which are preventing me from reaching enlightenment."

Next is the *strength of the antidote,* which is the actual method of purification and involves supplicating Guru Rinpoche with intense devotion while offering our confession to him. In response to the intensity of this devotion, nectar and rays of light emanate from Guru Rinpoche's heart and from his whole body. They dissolve into us and completely cleanse and purify all of our imperfections and negativities. Our body, purified, becomes immaculate and clear as crystal, filled with wisdom nectar. Guru Rinpoche, smiling radiantly, then speaks to us, saying, "All of your obscurations are purified." With this he melts into light and dissolves into us. We then remain for a while in a state of union with Guru Rinpoche's mind.

Fourth is the *strength of the promise.* After confessing, regretting, and purifying all our negative actions, we must then resolve firmly to refrain from committing such actions in the future, even at the cost of our lives. If this resolution or promise is not made, then confession is not of much use. If we think, "If the opportunity to commit this negative action arises in the future, I will be unable to refrain from repeating it," or if we think, "The committing of the fault is unimportant since I can easily purify it later on," then we will make little progress. Before we heard the teachings of the dharma, we were unaware of the dire effects of negative actions and negative emotions. Now, however, having a clear understanding of these things, we should make an unwavering promise to avoid such actions in the future.

According to the pith intructions, we can conclude our practice of the third branch by visualizing all our negative actions of body, speech, and mind in the form of a black substance that has gathered on the tip of our tongue. Then Guru Rinpoche emanates from his body rays of light that touch our tongue, completely dissolving all these gathered impurities in the same way that the rays of the morning sun dissolve the dew that has collected on the tips of the grass during the night. Thinking that everything has become cleansed, we realize the emptiness and clarity of the absolute state, the dharmakāya, which, being utterly free from duality, contains not the slightest trace of negativity. It is only due to our obscurations that we discriminate between pure and impure and are unable to recognize the void nature of phenomena. Thus, of all forms of confession, the ultimate one is to confess in the luminous expanse of dharmakāya, where there is no notion of subject, object, or action.

Rejoicing in Virtue

The fourth of the seven branches is rejoicing in virtue, the antidote for jealousy and hatred. Here we cultivate a deeply felt joy in all the positive and virtuous actions encompassed by the two truths. The virtuous actions celebrated on the relative level include the making of material offerings, *gaṇacakra* (the feast offerings), and offerings to the saṅgha, as well as prostrations and circumambulations of sacred sites. What is celebrated on the absolute level is deep contemplation, or samādhi. Virtuous actions performed on the relative level must be permeated or reinforced by the awareness of the absolute which flows from samādhi, in order for them to be effective.

The cultivation of positive actions must not be accompanied by feelings of self-satisfaction or pride; neither should we develop contempt for others whose positive actions fail to measure up to our own standards. We should never think that our offerings are the most profound and magnificent or that no one can match us in virtue. Even if we have accomplished virtuous actions of heroic proportions, such as the recitation of one hundred million Maṇi or Vajra Guru mantras, we may feel that we have done our best, but never that we have done enough. We should be like a wild yak: no matter how much grass it has consumed, it is always on the lookout for more. In the same way, no matter how great the number of our positive actions, we should always be eager to cultivate an even greater number of them. Any pride we might have because of our virtuous actions or any expectation that we might achieve fame through them will taint our actions and offerings, thus rendering them fruitless.

The virtuous actions of others should be a source of great joy. If we make offerings of great wealth and see someone else exceed our generosity, we might think his offering has greater merit than our own and thus feel irritated or annoyed. This is improper. Instead, we should think that he has made a very wonderful offering and sincerely wish that he might make an even greater one, rejoicing in this way without a trace of jealousy. Through such sincere joy in the accumulation of merit by others, arising in us free of envy and attachment, we ourselves accumulate equal merit. For example, King Prasenajit, having invited Lord Buddha and the entire saṅgha to stay on the palace grounds, provided sustenance for them all for an entire month. In the same city there lived an elderly woman, greatly devoted to the Buddha, who was very poor. At such a display of generosity, every day she thought with great joy in her heart, "How wonderful that the king thus accumulates such a vast heap of merit!" In his omniscience Lord Buddha knew of this. When at the end of the month he uttered the dedication of merit, to the surprise of everyone he did so in the name of this devout old woman.

We should always rejoice in a teacher expounding the dharma, benefiting beings, and seeing to it that temples and monasteries are built. We should rejoice if we see or hear of yogis deeply engaged in the practice of the development and completion stages and dwelling in solitude. We should rejoice at those who take the monastic vows of a novice or those of full ordination, thinking, "What excellent virtue! How marvelous that they are able to do such a thing!" and wishing that all beings might be able to do the same.

True positive action consists in the cultivation of virtue, never separate from the thought that its essence is dreamlike, illusory, and by nature void. By thus combining the two truths, our virtuous actions are free from clinging and attachment.

Requesting the Turning of the Wheel of Dharma

The fifth of the seven branches is requesting the turning of the wheel of dharma, the antidote for ignorance. Of all the activities of a buddha, the turning of the wheel of dharma is the most precious and fundamental. The verse says: "I urge you to turn the wheel of the dharma of the three vehicles." Though not found here, an additional verse can be added: "For the sake of the three classes of beings." For the benefit of beings of inferior faculties, the dharma is expounded through the teachings of the śrāvakas[35] and pratyekabuddhas, while for those of middling faculties it is expressed through the teachings of the Mahāyāna. For the benefit of beings of superior faculties, there are the teachings of the secret Mantrayāna. We should request fervently that the wheel of dharma of these three vehicles be turned.

When he attained enlightenment under the bodhi tree, Lord Buddha thoroughly understood the nature of all phenomena to be void. Having realized this, he felt that sentient beings, still ensnared in ignorance, would be unable to comprehend it. Thus he said, "I have found a nectarlike dharma, profound, peaceful, free from elaborations, luminous, and uncreated, but if I disclose it to others, they will not understand," and he remained in the absorption of deep samādhi for three weeks, thinking it useless to expound the dharma to other beings. The celestial beings, however, seeing that Śākyamuni had achieved buddhahood, realized that the benefit of sentient beings would not be furthered unless he could be persuaded to explain the dharma to them. Therefore, Indra, offering a conch shell that coiled to the right, and Brahmā, offering a thousand-spoked wheel of gold, together made the request that Lord Buddha come out of samādhi and turn the wheel of dharma. Yielding to their plea, Lord Buddha did so. Through having made this request, Indra and Brahmā accumulated boundless merit.

In the same way, we can now accumulate great merit by requesting teachings and by rejoicing when the teacher gives them, because through this sentient beings will be shown the path which dispels ignorance forever. Here we should visualize ourselves as emanating a great multiplicity of forms, monarchs, bodhisattvas, deities, and ordinary beings, each offering conch shells, golden wheels, and other precious things to the teacher, requesting that he turn the wheel of dharma for the benefit of beings.

Requesting the Teacher to Remain in This World

The sixth branch is requesting that the teacher remain. The verse says: "I supplicate you not to pass into *nirvāṇa* until saṃsāra is completely emptied, but to stay in this world to continue to benefit beings." If in this world there were no buddhas or spiritual friends or teachers, then our precious human body, with all its freedoms, faculties, and intelligence, would be engaged only in the activities and schemes of saṃsāra. We would spend all our time protecting our loved ones, vanquishing our enemies, and striving to accumulate wealth, fame, and power. There is no benefit in this. We would be unaware of the suffering in the lower realms and their cause, unaware of the endless chain of future rebirths and of what to cultivate and what to avoid. Therefore, visualizing ourselves as the lay disciple Chanda, who by his request extended Lord Buddha's life by three months, we should pray that the teachers remain until all sentient beings have been rescued from the wheel of saṃsāric existence.

Dedicating the Merit

The verse of the seventh and last branch, the dedication of merit, says: "I dedicate all the merit I have accumulated throughout the three times for the attainment of great enlightenment." Whatever merit has been accumulated through the practice of the first six branches, as well as whatever virtuous actions we have performed in the past and will perform in the future, we dedicate to all sentient beings. We dedicate the merit with the wish: "May all the infinity of sentient beings use this merit as a foundation for the attainment of enlightenment. Through this may all beings be freed from the lower realms and be established on the path of liberation." It is important for us to make the dedication on as vast a scale as possible. In this way we emulate the great bodhisattvas like Samantabhadra and Mañjuśrī when they dedicate the merit of their activities for the benefit of all beings. The dedication should be completely free from any hope of reward. As much as we can, we should free ourselves from clinging to the idea of an actor, an action, and an object of action, realizing these three to be just empty concepts.

If we are doing the *ngöndro,* or preliminary practice, it is especially appropriate to do the prostrations in conjunction with guru yoga, while reciting the seven-branch prayer. This is because prostrations, mandala offering, and confession are more effective when focused on our guru. A single prostration made to our guru is more powerful than one hundred thousand prostrations to the buddhas and bodhisattvas of the ten directions of space. This is why we make the seven-branch offering directly to our teacher, for through this all our obscurations will be dispelled, all the blessings of the teacher will swiftly enter our being, and we will thus be able to perfect the accumulations of merit and wisdom. If we collect and concentrate rainfall into a single large funnel, we can fill a large barrel very quickly. In the same way, if we concentrate all our efforts by offering them to the teacher, we will be able to make very rapid progress on the path.

We must always seal our practice by dedicating whatever merit we have accumulated for the benefit and liberation of all sentient beings. Merit that has been dedicated will never be lost, just as a drop of water placed in the ocean will never evaporate. Merit that has not been dedicated will produce only ephemeral results, just as a drop of water placed on a hot stone will evaporate instantaneously.

Devotion and Prayer

Guru yoga is a method or skillful means for generating in ourselves the fervent devotion that enables us effortlessly to see the guru as the Buddha himself. At first this devotion may not be natural or spontaneous, so we must employ a variety of techniques to help us achieve this. Chiefly we must always remember the excellent qualities of the teacher, especially his kindness to us. By repeatedly generating confidence, appreciation in the guru, and devotion toward him, a time will come when the mere mention of his name or the thought of him will stop all our ordinary perceptions, and we will see him as the Buddha himself.

The verse that we use in addressing our prayer of devotion to Guru Rinpoche says:

> Please listen to me, precious Guru Rinpoche. You are the most precious, most glorious embodiment of the compassion and blessings of all the buddhas. You are the sole protector and lord of all sentient beings. Without any hesitation or restraint, I offer you my possessions, my body, my lungs, my heart, my chest, my very being. I offer you myself completely. Until I reach enlightenment, no matter what happiness or suffering I may encounter, you, great precious one, the Lotus-Born Guru,

know everything about me. I have no other hope
but you; I am in your hands.

[*At this point we recite the Vajra Guru mantra three hundred times.*]

Why do we make this prayer to Guru Rinpoche? Why is he the one to whom we turn? Ordinary people tend to rely on the person who has the greatest influence and power. So here we rely on Guru Rinpoche, who is the union of all the buddhas and bodhisattvas who dwell in the countless buddha-fields throughout the ten directions. He is the gathering of all their excellent qualities, ability, and power to benefit beings. In this universe, he displayed an absolute and unchallengeable mastery of all the techniques and accomplishments of the secret Mantrayāna. In this light, it is to him that we turn in this age when the negative and poisonous emotions of sentient beings are extremely gross. Famine, epidemics, and wars prevail, and even those few who turn their minds toward the dharma find terrible obstacles blocking their progress and preventing the attainment of the ultimate goal.

Guru Rinpoche, in his omniscience, foresaw all this, and out of his limitless compassion he provided effective methods for beings in this era. As he himself is uniquely endowed to help us, we can rely on him with unwavering confidence. As he said, "Whoever meditates on me meditates on all the buddhas. Whoever sees me sees all the buddhas. I am the union of all *sugata*s, the 'ones gone to bliss.'"

On the outer level, his body is the saṅgha, his speech the dharma, and his mind the Buddha. On the inner level, his body is the lama, his speech the yidam, and his mind the ḍākinī. On the secret level, the level of the three kāyas, his manifested body is the nirmāṇakāya, in the aspect of

Padmasambhava, the Lotus-Born Guru. His speech is the sambhogakāya, in the aspect of Avalokiteśvara, the buddha of infinite compassion. His mind is the dharmakāya, in the aspect of Amitābha, the buddha of boundless light. From this we can see that Guru Rinpoche is, in fact, the very quintessence of all the buddhas. His vast buddha activity is manifested most clearly to us through the fact that to beings like us, tormented by ignorance, he has revealed the precious instructions on what to adopt and what to avoid on the path. This will allow us to travel the path of enlightenment to its end.

Guru Rinpoche turns the wheel of dharma unceasingly. In his speech aspect, Guru Rinpoche being the source of all dharma, there is not a single one among the infinity of tantras and secret teachings in the universe that is not known and mastered by him. At present, we who inhabit this Jambudvīpa, or earth, are not fortunate enough to see him face to face. Although he is no longer manifesting as a body visible to ordinary people, he is present in all of his teachings. To preserve them for the sake of future generations and ensure their potency and freshness, he transmitted them to his closest disciples and then concealed them in the form of *termas*, or "spiritual treasures." As these disciples took successive rebirths, they rediscovered the various treasures hidden by Guru Rinpoche in rocks, in lakes, in the sky, and within their minds. By rediscovering the termas at precisely the time when they would be of the most benefit, it was guaranteed that the treasures would not be distorted over the long process of transmission from generation to generation. Hence the terma tradition is called the short lineage.

If we practice these properly, with the requisite devotion and sincerity, there is no doubt that we will be able to achieve the common and supreme accomplishments. These teachings and the opportunity to practice them are offered to us like the vast array of possibilities in a large city. It is up to us to use them or not.

Fervent prayers to Guru Rinpoche will shut the doors that lead to rebirth in lower realms and, setting us firmly on the path to deliverance from saṃsāra, will eventually result in our achievement of enlightenment. Thus the guru, glorious Vajradhara, is the root of all blessings, through which everything can be accomplished.

From the primordial buddha, Samantabhadra, down to ourselves, the profound teachings have been transmitted through an unbroken lineage of enlightened beings. There are three kinds of transmission, which correspond to the different levels of beings. The highest level, mind to mind, was given by Samantabhadra to the buddhas of the five families. The middle-level transmission, that of the *vidyādharas*, or awareness-holders, is given by symbolic gesture or utterance. The last level, the ear-whispered oral transmission, is for individuals like ourselves.

Guru Rinpoche himself received and can transmit all three levels of transmission. Since he possesses the full wisdom, compassion, and ability of all the buddhas, he has mastery of the wisdom-mind lineage.

Manifesting in this universe in the form of a holder of the adamantine wisdom, Guru Rinpoche traveled throughout all the sacred lands receiving teachings from all the great teachers, including the eight vidyādharas of India. In particular he received from Śrī Siṃha the empowerment of the "efflorescence of awareness." He was able to receive and realize all these teachings through gesture and utterance, and thus he holds the lineage of symbolic transmission.

Never having to train or study, he received and was

able to master instantly all the instructions and all the levels of meaning of the various classes of tantras of the secret Mantrayāna. Thus he holds the complete ear-whispered transmission. Having traveled to all the buddha-fields, he received the teachings of all the buddhas.

Also complete within Guru Rinpoche are the three roots. As the lama, or root of blessings, he holds the three lineages, as we have just seen. He is also the yidam, or root of accomplishment, and the ḍākinī, or root of activity.

In addition, the mandalas of the body, speech, mind, qualities, and activities of all the buddhas are complete in him. In the aspect of body, he is Yamāntaka; in the aspect of speech, he is Hayagrīva; in the aspect of mind, he is Yangdak Heruka; and in the aspect of activity, he is Vajrakīlaya. Guru Rinpoche can, according to his wish, emanate the one hundred and eight peaceful and wrathful deities, displaying the entire mandala, or he can gather an infinity of deities and absorb them into himself. He is Amitābha, he is Amitāyus, he is Avalokiteśvara, he is Ārya Tārā, he is Vajrasattva, he is the thousand buddhas, he is the eight manifestations, he is the twenty-five disciples, he is the eighty-four mahasiddhas, he is the gurus of the eight streams of the teachings, he is our own root teacher. The scope of his activities and his power are such that simply by meditating on him we can attain full buddhahood.

Guru Rinpoche is also the sovereign of all the ḍākinīs and protectors of the dharma, who themselves are the root of all activity. Throughout the three places,[36] the mere sound of his name arouses the ḍākas and ḍākinīs to perceive him as their lord and to offer him the whole oceanlike expanse of the tantras of the secret Mantrayāna. At his command, the ḍākas and ḍākinīs will clear the path of obstacles, enabling us to make rapid progress.

He does not hide within him the treasure of his wondrous qualities; his ever-flowing compassion is the compassion of all the buddhas, and his ability to help beings is equal to theirs. In this decadent age, when nothing remains but degenerate traces of the original perfections, when the blessings of the deities, celestial beings, and all dharmas seem to be vanishing, those of Guru Rinpoche are in fact shining more brilliantly than ever before. His unceasing compassionate activity, rather than being diminished in this dark age, has become even more swift and sure.

We say that Guru Rinpoche is the lord or protector of all sentient beings because all turn to him for refuge. Beings afflicted by poisonous emotions and accumulated karma who turn their minds toward him will receive his compassion and his blessings. Realizing this, we can wholeheartedly offer him whatever we hold most dear—our body, our loved ones, our possessions, and the very depth of our being—without the slightest hesitation. We make such an offering completely free from any second thoughts, giving him everything with utter finality, like a stone thrown into water. Even if we were able to offer all the gold contained in the entire universe, we should feel it insufficient. No offering, no matter how immense, could ever be enough to repay the kindness of Guru Rinpoche.

From this point in our lives until we reach his level of attainment, through our practice on the path, all the positive things that happen to us, all the signs and realizations, all the purification of our defects, all the benefits of good health, long life, and prosperity, are due to the kindness of Guru Rinpoche. Whatever good things we may experience should be offered freely to the guru, without any clinging. Whatever unfavorable circumstances may befall us, whether illness, material loss, harsh criticism, or unjust imprisonment, we should also attribute to the kindness of the guru, for through our misfortunes we will be able to cleanse ourselves of accumulated negative karma. We should never think, "I have prayed to Guru Rinpoche so much, I have practiced so intensively, how could these things ever happen to me?" Rather, we should be able to use our suffering on the path, by taking upon ourselves all the suffering of other sentient beings.

We must realize that from now on, whatever we experience, both good and bad, is in the hands of Guru Rinpoche. Whether we roam through the buddha-fields drinking from the teachings of the buddhas and bodhisattvas or roam through the endless suffering of saṃsāra, we should think, "Guru Rinpoche, you know everything that happens to me. I am in your hands."

If we are able to develop this degree of confidence in him, then Guru Rinpoche will be for us like the ground on which we walk, always supporting us. From this total confidence, all the qualities and benefits will arise naturally. Unobstructed by obstacles, we will be free from sickness and suffering, we will enjoy a long life, and all our aspirations will be fulfilled. Yet these are only minor blessings. More important, this confidence will give rise to experiences and realization, it will permit us to achieve the level of the great vidyādharas of India and of the twenty-five chief disciples of Guru Rinpoche in Tibet. These are major blessings.

With all this in mind we should pray fervently, saying:

> I have no object of hope but you. In this decadent age, when all beings are sinking in the swamp of unbearable suffering, protect them from all this, O great guru. You who are endowed with wisdom and grace and waves of blessing, grant the four initiations. You who are endowed with compassion,

enhance my realization. You who are endowed with ability, purify the two obscurations. You in whom I place my hopes, establish me on the path toward enlightenment. Through you may all the blessings of the buddhas enter my mindstream. I pray to you now with my whole being. You, in your omniscience, can see that I have taken birth in this decadent age, full of disease and strife, when sentient beings are violent, proud, and arrogant, lacking diligence in the practice of dharma, and always seeking what is unwholesome. In such an age, attachment, anger, stupidity, illness, famine, and war are always increasing; here we are experiencing the fruits of our karma. Like a madman happy to walk into a fire, we happily accumulate the seeds of our future suffering. Like a blind man without a guide or a madman without a keeper, we are utterly sunk in the mire of suffering without even realizing it. You, Guru Rinpoche, can protect me from wandering aimlessly in this inferior, vile wilderness. Please bestow upon me the vajra wisdom of your body, speech, and mind, and grant me the four initiations so that I may realize the profound meaning of the Great Perfection. Through your compassion, may my realization increase, and may you kindle within me the wisdom of the natural state.[37]

[*At this point, we recite the Vajra Guru mantra three hundred times.*]

When realization takes birth in our being, the two veils—both the one that darkens our minds through negative emotions and the one that obscures knowledge of the relative and the absolute—will be lifted and vanish. We should pray with full confidence that Guru Rinpoche will quickly grant his blessings and that he will reveal to us the meaning of the Great Perfection.

> I pray to you from the bottom of my heart, not simply with my lips, to grant your blessings so that all my aspirations may be fulfilled.

While making this prayer, we should think, "Guru Rinpoche, I am not just mouthing words. I am not begging for your protection in this life and in the bardo to flatter you, but am praying to you from the very core of my being, from the marrow of my bones. I have no other thought but you. I remember nothing but you. I want to disappear into you like a stone thrown into water. I cannot bear to be separate from you."

In this way, our mind becomes completely filled with the presence of the guru. All negative thoughts, no matter how gross or poisonous, become completely pacified and vanish at the very thought of the guru. We should pray with all the energy and intensity at our disposal until we are blessed with this kind of experience. If we actually develop such genuine devotion, then Guru Rinpoche will be like a mother who always has the greatest love for her child. Whenever such a mother wants to give her child something, she never thinks, "Oh, this is too good for him." Rather, she always gives the best things that she can find. We should pray to Guru Rinpoche, thinking, "Please grant me your compassion and deliver me from suffering in this and future lives. Please guide me to the higher realms and help me to attain ultimate enlightenment."

[*With our minds thus filled with total devotion, here again we recite the Vajra Guru mantra as much as possible —at least four hundred times.*]

Vajra Guru Mantra

Why is it so important to recite mantras, and what are they? Just as we visualize ourselves as a deity and the surroundings as a buddha-field in order to purify our impure perception of form, we recite mantras to purify our impure perception of sound. *Mantra* is a Sanskrit word that means "to protect the mind," since, while reciting mantras, the mind is protected from its ordinary deluded thoughts.

The mantra most intimately associated with Guru Rinpoche is known as the Vajra Guru mantra: OṂ ĀḤ HŪNG VAJRA-GURU-PADMA-SIDDHI HŪNG. This mantra is the life and heart, the quintessence of Guru Rinpoche; it is, in fact, Guru Rinpoche in the form of sound.

Oṃ

The first syllable, OṂ, corresponds to the body aspect of all the buddhas. Although Guru Rinpoche is the all-pervading lord of the five buddha families,[38] the OṂ in this instance corresponds particularly to the Buddha Amitābha, who is the dharmakāya aspect of the lotus family.

Āḥ

The second syllable, ĀḤ, corresponds to the speech aspect of all the buddhas. In this case it refers specifically to the Bodhisattva Avalokiteśvara, the Great Compassionate One, who is the sambhogakāya aspect of the lotus family. From the syllable ĀḤ emanate the eighty-four thousand sections of the dharma.

Hūng

The third syllable, HŪNG, corresponds to the mind aspect or wisdom essence of all the buddhas, which here manifests as the Lotus-Born Guru and corresponds to the nirmāṇakāya aspect of the lotus family. Guru Rinpoche is in fact the complete union of the three kāyas, and the first three syllables of his mantra indicate this.

Vajra Guru

Next comes VAJRA GURU. *Vajra*, a Sanskrit word, pronounced *benzar* in Tibetan, refers to the diamond (Tib. *rdo-rje*, the "lord of stones"), supreme among natural materials. The diamond is so hard that nothing can cut through it, and this quality permits it to cut through anything. In the same way, the unchanging wisdom nature of Guru Rinpoche's body, speech, and mind cannot be harmed by delusions and poisonous emotions, while his body, speech, mind, and wisdom effortlessly annihilate the obscurations and delusions that are the karmic result of negative emotions and negative actions. So we may understand that by *vajra guru* (or *dorje lama* in Tibetan) we mean a great, accomplished being who has attained the ultimate end of the path of the Vajrayāna. In short, *vajra* indicates absolute mastery or realization of the indivisibility of the three kāyas.

As we mentioned before, translated literally from the Sanskrit, *guru* means "heavy" and implies that the guru is heavy with good qualities. Since the body, speech, and mind of Guru Rinpoche possess an infinity of qualities identical with those of all the buddhas, we can consider them as the precious contents of an enormous treasure chest filled to overflowing—such a chest would be quite heavy, and this is what is meant by "heavy with good qualities." Just as gold is both heavy and precious, the guru is the heaviest and most precious of all beings because of his inconceivable and flawless qualities. The Tibetan word for guru is *lama,* which connotes something lofty or above all things in excellence. For instance, in paying homage to the three jewels, the three roots, or the three kāyas, or in the recitation of the names of the buddhas, we always begin with the word *lama* to indicate that what follows is unsurpassed and unsurpassable.

We refer to our teacher as lama because, having the good fortune to meet him in this life and to hear his instructions, we thereafter remember him at all times with great devotion. We will then always remain beyond the reach of negative emotions, never falling prey to the various karmas and obscurations of saṃsāra.

From the moment of his appearance on the northwest border of Oḍḍiyāṇa until the moment of his departure for the southeastern continent of the *rākṣasa*s, Guru Rinpoche displayed and taught all aspects of the sutras and tantras. But since he primarily unfolded the secret teachings of the Vajrayāna, through which one can attain both the ordinary and supreme accomplishments in a single lifetime, we refer to him as dorje lama, or vajra guru. It was to teach the Vajrayāna that Guru Rinpoche manifested in our world. When Lord Buddha turned the wheel of dharma in India, in accordance with the needs and capacities of the beings there, he did not teach the Vajrayāna very extensively.

As the moment approached when Lord Buddha was about to pass into *parinirvāṇa,* the Riksum Gönpo, or three protectors—Mañjuśrī, Avalokiteśvara, and Vajrapāṇi—appeared before him and said: "Please turn the wheel of Vajrayāna and in this way benefit the beings of the Land of Snow." They then pleaded with him to remain on this earth in order to fulfill their request. In response, Lord Buddha told them that after his parinirvāṇa, another, greater manifestation would appear, born in an immaculate way, in order to propagate the profound teachings; and that they themselves—particularly Avalokiteśvara—would be entrusted to safeguard the spreading of dharma in Tibet. In this way he announced the coming of the Lotus-Born Guru.

According to ordinary history, Lord Buddha did not unfold and expound the teachings of the secret Vajrayāna. However, at the moment of his parinirvāṇa, five of his greatest disciples who had gathered together on the Blazing Iron Mountain perceived his passing through their powers of clairvoyance. These were the five remarkable beings, vidyādharas, respectively, of the realms of celestial beings, rākṣasas, *yakṣas*, *nāgas*, and humans.

"Now the teacher is no more in this world," they lamented. "Who will dispel the darkness of ignorance? Who will show us what is to be practiced and what is to be avoided?" In response to their deep sorrow and fervent supplication, Vajrasattva emanated from the hearts of all the buddhas in the form of Vajrapāṇi. He revealed and explained the secret Mantrayāna to them. Shortly thereafter, the teachings of Mahāyoga, in the form of the eighteen classes of the tantras of the Magical Net of Emanation, fell from the sky onto the roof of the palace of King Indrabodhi, and the teachings of Anuyoga manifested themselves in the land of Siṃhala. Then Garab Dorje, the first human being in the lineage of the Great Perfection, began to teach and elucidate the practices of Atiyoga. These three great rivers of wisdom flow into the vast ocean of the teachings of Guru

Rinpoche. Though encompassing the complete knowledge and profundity of the sutras, his teachings chiefly emphasize the path of the secret Vajrayāna.

Padma

Padma, the Sanskrit term for lotus, is pronounced *pema* in Tibetan. There are five buddha families—*buddha, vajra, ratna, padma*, and *karma*—and these are represented by the five buddhas: Vairocana, Akṣobhya, Ratnasambhava, Amitābha, and Amoghasiddhi, respectively. Because the Lotus-Born Guru is the nirmāṇakāya emanation of Amitābha, belonging to the lotus family, his initial name is Padma. Thus, in his mantra, in light of what we have just explained, we call him Vajra Guru Padma.

Siddhi Hūng

At the end of the mantra we say "SIDDHI HŪNG." SIDDHI refers to both kinds of accomplishments—the ordinary and the supreme—while HŪNG is a syllable of invocation requesting that Guru Rinpoche grant us these two accomplishments. Freedom from illness and possession of all endowments, such as prosperity and long life, are among the ordinary or mundane accomplishments. The supreme accomplishment is to attain the level of realization of Guru Rinpoche himself. So, in brief, the whole mantra can be said to mean: "You, the Vajra Guru, who arose from a lotus, please grant me the ordinary and supreme accomplishments."

The Vajra Guru mantra has twelve syllables. With respect to our present condition of delusion and impurity, these syllables correspond to the twelve interdependent links of origination, which rise from ignorance and culminate in rebirth, and through the operation of which we wander in saṃsāra. When these links or factors are purified, they correspond to the twelve branches of Lord Buddha's teaching.[39] Furthermore, in these twelve syllables of Guru Rinpoche's mantra are condensed the mantras of all the gurus, all the yidams, and all the ḍākinīs.

The Lotus-Born Guru and his mantra are inseparable. When we utter this mantra, which includes the name of the guru, it is like repeatedly calling on someone whose response is unfailing. If we pray, reciting his mantra one-pointedly, there is no doubt whatsoever that Guru Rinpoche will turn his compassion toward us and grant his blessings.

We should recite this mantra with our entire being, free from hypocrisy, distraction, or any kind of mechanical repetitiveness. We should not feel that we have accomplished any great thing if we have managed to recite the Vajra Guru mantra a few hundred or a few thousand times. In fact, our recitation of this mantra should be uninterrupted, like the constant flow of a river, and should become one with our breath. As we recite the mantra we should at the same time visualize that we are receiving the four initiations from Guru Rinpoche.

There is no recitation superior to that of the Vajra Guru, Guru Rinpoche's mantra. We should make strenuous efforts in the practice of this recitation, remembering Guru Rinpoche with unwavering devotion. At the end of each session we should think that all sentient beings, transformed into light, rise swiftly up to dissolve into Guru Rinpoche's heart. While reciting the Sangdopalri prayer, we should wish fervently that all beings be reborn in the paradise of Sangdopalri, the Glorious Copper-Colored Mountain.

Receiving the Four Empowerments

By now we have learned how to visualize ourselves as Vajrayoginī with Guru Rinpoche above our head, how to invite the wisdom deities from the buddha-field, and how the deities dissolve into us. We have learned about the accumulation of merit through the offering of the Seven-Branch Prayer and the various ways to generate faith and devotion in our recitation of the Vajra Guru mantra. Now, for the conclusion, we must learn how to receive the four empowerments from Guru Rinpoche and the assembly of great beings who compose his retinue.

The Sanskrit word that we translate into English as "empowerment" is *abhiṣeka,* which means both to rend and to fill. The abhiṣeka rends or tears away the veils of ignorance and fills us with the blessings of the body, speech, and mind of the guru. We speak of this as an empowerment because through it we become empowered to cultivate particular spiritual practices that will ultimately blossom into realization. Thus the empowerment is both a permission and a blessing. To practice without having received an empowerment is like trying to extract oil by squeezing sand. We must first receive the empowerment from a qualified teacher, and then we can renew it again and again through the practice of guru yoga.

In order to receive the four empowerments, we must turn our mind toward Guru Rinpoche with a fierce and yearning devotion. In response, Guru Rinpoche will turn his wisdom mind toward us with great compassion and loving-kindness. At this point we may include the prayer addressed to all the buddhas and gurus of the Longchen Nyingthig lineage, which begins with the words "*Emaho!* In the limitless and all-encompassing buddha-field . . ."

and which can be found in the more expanded version of this guru yoga within the Longchen Nyingthig ngöndro itself. At the end of this prayer, all the yidams, ḍākas, ḍākinīs, great beings, and protectors who constitute his retinue melt into light and dissolve in Guru Rinpoche. Now even more radiant and resplendent than before, ablaze with blessings, Guru Rinpoche abides as the sovereign union of all the buddhas. It is from him that we now receive the empowerments.

Between Guru Rinpoche's eyebrows, in the center of his forehead, we visualize a white letter OṂ, which like a crystal radiates very intense, brilliant rays of white light. As we visualize ourselves as Vajrayoginī, these are absorbed into a corresponding white OṂ on our own forehead, and these completely pervade our entire body, coursing through all the subtle veins or channels, purifying all the negative actions of the body.

There are three main channels: the *uma*, or central channel; the *roma*, or right channel; and the *kyangma*, or left channel. These channels run from below the navel to the crown of the head, through the five *cakra*s, or "wheels." At the forehead is the cakra of great bliss; at the throat is the cakra of enjoyment; at the heart is the cakra of dharmas or phenomena; at the navel is the cakra of formation; and at the secret center is the bliss-preserving cakra. From these cakras many smaller channels radiate laterally like the spokes of a wheel. In our current state of obscuration and delusion, the karmic energies (Tib. *lung,* "winds") that bind us to cyclic existence run throughout these various channels. In order for us to emerge from delusion, these energies must be purified and transmuted into wisdom energy.

When we receive the blessings, which stream out as

rays of light from Guru Rinpoche's forehead center into our own, all the impurities in these channels are cleansed. At the same time, we receive the blessings of the vajra body of Guru Rinpoche.

The first of the four empowerments or initiations is the *vase initiation*, which we normally receive from the teacher while visualizing the main deity and the whole mandala as being within the vase used during the empowerment ritual. The mandala then melts into nectar, which completely fills the vase, and we receive the blessings from this vase. In this case, through the absorption of the rays of light into our foreheads, we renew this first initiation. Through it, we are empowered to do the various meditations, sādhanas, and visualizations of the development stage, such as those involving the peaceful and wrathful deities. Through this blessing, the seed for becoming a *vidyādhara of total maturation* is planted within us. By vidyādhara we mean one whose mind has matured into wisdom. Although his body remains as an envelope made of the five aggregates, it is ready to dissolve into the wisdom body at the moment of death. From the perspective of the five paths, this corresponds to the paths of accumulation and of joining. The auspicious connection necessary for achievement of the nirmāṇakāya, the manifested body of the buddha, is established within us with this first initiation.

Next, from the throat center of Guru Rinpoche, we visualize a red letter ĀḤ. Brilliant rays of light stream forth from this, as if from an incandescent, blazing ruby. These rays are absorbed into our own throat center, where we have visualized a corresponding letter ĀḤ. This red light pours into our body, pervading and cleansing all our channels, thus purifying all negative actions committed through speech, such as lies, slander, idle chatter, and harsh words.

It also purifies the karmic energies on which the negative actions of speech ride. At the same time, we receive the blessing of Guru Rinpoche's vajra speech, as well as the second or *secret initiation*, normally given by the teacher from the skull cup filled with amṛita, the nectar of immortality. With this we are empowered to perform the various recitations, and we receive the seed for attaining the level of the *vidyādhara who has power over life*. This is the level at which both mind and body are transmuted into wisdom and the auspicious connection enabling us to achieve the sambhogakāya level is established in our being.

Then, at Guru Rinpoche's heart center, we visualize a letter HŪNG, blue as the clear azure of an autumn sky, radiating dazzling light, which is absorbed into the HŪNG at our own heart center. Again, this light pervades our body and courses through all the channels, purifying the three negative actions of mind—envy, malice, and wrong views. It also purifies the white and red essences, or *thigle*, which form the support of the mind. At this time we receive the blessings of the vajra mind of Guru Rinpoche, as well as the third or *wisdom initiation*. This we normally receive while visualizing that countless rays of light, emanating from the bodies of all the deities of the mandala, are absorbed into us. This enables us to realize the wisdom of great bliss, achieve the level of dharmakāya, and become a *mahāmudrā vidyādhara*. When Guru Rinpoche bestowed the empowerment of Vajrakīlaya upon his disciples, he assumed the form of Vajrakīlaya at the center of his mandala. Such capacity for the limitless display of wisdom forms is the fruit or characteristic of this level of vidyādhara, called *mahāmudrā* because *mahā* means "great" and *mudrā* means "display."

Now a second blue letter HŪNG emerges from the

HŪNG at Guru Rinpoche's heart center and, like a shooting star, penetrates our own heart center to blend indissolubly with our own mind, filling our whole body with light. This completely purifies both the subtle defilements of body, speech, and mind that mask realization and the deluded ground of defilements itself, the *kunshi.* Called the *ālaya-vijñāna* in Sanskrit, this is in effect the storehouse of all habitual tendencies, as well as all positive and negative karma. Of the two veils, this initiation tears away the one that obscures gnosis or ultimate knowledge. This veil is the result of conceiving of a subject, action, and object, termed in Tibetan as the *three encircling concepts.* Through this initiation we also receive the blessing of Guru Rinpoche's body, speech, and mind taken as a unity.

This fourth or *word initiation* is the introduction to the natural state of all phenomena; through it we become a proper vessel for the practice of Dzogchen, the Great Perfection. The seed is also sown within us for the attainment of the level of the *spontaneously accomplished vidyādhara,* which permits the spontaneous accomplishment of the five kāyas,[40] the level of Guru Rinpoche himself. It is the ultimate buddhahood, the indivisibility of the three kāyas, or the *svabhāvikakāya,* the body of the true nature. At this point our body, speech, and mind become inseparable and of one taste with the body, speech, and mind of Guru Rinpoche. Then, remaining in equanimity, in this state of one taste, we continue the recitation of the mantra. This is called "seeing the true face of the absolute guru." If we thus realize that our mind is the dharmakāya, it is the same as having received the empowerment of all the buddhas of the past, present, and future.

Five levels can be recognized in the practice of guru yoga. The outer level, for accumulating merit, includes visualizing the guru and his retinue in the space before one, taking refuge, generating bodhicitta, offering the seven branches, and so forth, while keeping in mind that deities are simply the display of the guru's wisdom mind. The inner level, for purifying one's perceptions, involves visualizing the guru above one's head and receiving his blessings. The secret level, for letting wisdom arise all at once in one's being, involves visualizing the guru in one's heart. The most secret level, in which one recognizes the deity as oneself, involves visualizing oneself as a yidam deity, realizing that one's body, speech, and mind have always been inseparable from the body, speech and mind of the guru, and arise in the form of the deity. In the absolute level, having blended one's mind with the mind of the guru, one realizes the ultimate nature of the guru, the absolute void expanse devoid of concepts and conditions, and remains effortlessly in this inconceivable luminous wisdom.

Transference at Death

After the four initiations, and before concluding the practice, we pray with this verse:

> When my life comes to its end,
> My primordial form, Vajrayoginī,
> Transforming into a bright sphere of light
> And having merged inseparably with the Precious
>   One Born from the Lotus,
> May I attain buddhahood, the state of great union,
> In the self-appearing Glorious Mountain of
>   Ngayap,
> The nondual emanated buddha-field.

This refers to the moment of death. All phenomena and perceptions of this life vanish, while those of the next life begin to dawn. Caught unaware by the lord of death, we cannot be sure that we will be spared great suffering in our future lives. Therefore, we should supplicate Guru Rinpoche fervently:

> Guru Rinpoche, at this moment of death please look upon me with your great compassion. Without your constant kindness, freedom from wandering in the confusion of *saṃsāra* will never come!

Still visualizing ourselves as Vajrayoginī, as we supplicate with fierce devotion, Guru Rinpoche looks down at us with great loving-kindness and smiles. From his heart center emanates beams of red light, bright as the rising sun, warm with blessings, and filled with compassion and bliss. These dissolve into our own hearts. This light is like a messenger coming to invite and lead us to the Glorious Copper-Colored Mountain. We then melt into light and dissolve gradually from the top of our head and the soles of our feet toward our own heart center, becoming a small sphere of brilliant red light, which then shoots skyward. This ball of red light, which is like the quintessence of our devotion, leaps, soaring into the sky to dissolve into the guru's heart. Then Guru Rinpoche himself, like a rainbow vanishing in the sky, dissolves into light and merges with the absolute expanse. We then remain in a nondual state, without distinction between the mind of the guru and our own. If we can, we should abide in this natural simplicity, in a state where we neither follow thoughts that arise nor try to prevent their arising. Of all the ways to conclude the guru yoga practice, this is the foremost. This is also the most profound and essential way of performing *phowa*, the transference of consciousness, at the moment of death: if we are suddenly or unexpectedly confronted with our own death, we should clearly visualize ourselves dissolving into the guru's heart and our mind merging with the guru's mind.

This is the completion stage aspect of this guru yoga. We then repeat the last verse of the prayer we said before:

> I pray to you from the bottom of my heart, not simply with my lips, to grant blessings from the vast expanse of your heart so that all my aspirations may be fulfilled.

Guru Rinpoche's mind and ours become one, and we remain for a while in a state of bliss-void untainted by mental fabrications—the natural simplicity of the guru's mind.

When we arise from that state, we should perceive all appearances as the manifestation of the guru, all sounds as mantra, and all thoughts as the display of wisdom. Then, with great love and compassion, we should dedicate the merit of our practice to all beings without exception and bring to all our activities the understanding we have acquired during this practice. For the dedication we can use the prayers found in the expanded ngöndro or preliminary practices of the Longchen Nyingthig.

In general we should, at all times, again and again, make vast prayers for the sake of all beings, praying, "May the teachers live long; may the teachings remain for a long time and spread all over the universe; may I be of infinite benefit to beings and to the teachings." When falling asleep we should think, "May all beings achieve the absolute state"; when waking up, "May all beings awake into the enlightened state"; when getting up, "May all beings obtain the body of a buddha"; when putting on clothes, "May all beings have modesty and a sense of shame"; when lighting a fire, "May all beings burn the wood of disturbing emotions"; when eating, "May all beings eat the food of samādhi"; when opening a door, "May all beings open the door to the city of liberation"; when closing the door, "May all beings close the door to the lower realms"; when going outside, "May I set out on the path to free all beings"; when walking uphill, "May I take all beings to the higher realms"; when walking downhill, "May I go to free beings from the lower realms"; when seeing happiness, "May all beings achieve the happiness of buddhahood"; when seeing suffering, "May the suffering of all beings be pacified." It is said that the way we will eventually be able to benefit beings depends on the magnitude of the prayers we have made while on the path. One of these prayers, composed by Gyalwa Longchenpa, says:

> In all my lives, wherever I am born,
> May I obtain the seven noble qualities of the
> higher realms.
> On being born, may I meet the dharma
> And have the freedom to practice it in the right
> way.
> Then, pleasing the holy lama,
> May I practice the dharma day and night.
> Having realized the dharma and achieved its
> essential purpose,
> In that life, may I cross over the ocean of
> existence.
> Teaching the holy dharma to the world,
> May I never tire of accomplishing the benefit of
> others.
> Through the great wave of impartial benefit to
> others,
> May all beings attain buddhahood together.

Thus it is essential to seal our practice by dedicating the merit along with vast aspirations.

Making the Practice Part of One's Life

In general, by the term "dharma practitioner" we mean a person who is able to handle all kinds of circumstances, both good and bad, one who can take even the worst experiences as catalysts to help further progress in his or her practice. The circumstances in which we find ourselves should actually clarify our practice, our experiences, and our realization, and we should be able to understand all situations, both favorable and unfavorable, as teachings on the path.

The obstacles that can arise from both good and bad circumstances should never deter us or dominate us. We should be like the earth, which supports all living beings, without regard to distinctions of good or bad, favorable or unfavorable. The earth simply abides. When faced with difficult situations, a practitioner should use them as an opportunity to strengthen his practice, just as a strong wind, rather than extinguishing a bonfire, intensifies it and causes it to blaze even more brightly.

Should we encounter unfortunate circumstances, such as bad influences, harsh words, criticism, or even being thrown into prison, we should not think: "I have prayed so much to the three jewels; I do not deserve such treatment." We should understand that all such difficulties arise as a result of having harmed others throughout our past lives, and we should endure sufferings and hardships, thinking, "Through what has befallen me, may the suffering of other beings, caused by the negative actions they have accumulated in their past lives, all be condensed and exhausted in me." We should always realize that our trying circumstances are actually a manifestation of the skillful means of Guru Rinpoche, who in this way gives us occasions to purify our negative karma.

Thus, we should cheerfully accept any suffering or criticism, thinking, "This has been given to me out of the great kindness of my teacher." For example, many Tibetans, while suffering severe deprivation and imprisonment throughout the past twenty-five years in Tibet, never wavered in their great devotion to the teacher and sincere enthusiasm for dharma practice. In this case, their experience of extreme suffering had turned their minds toward the dharma and strengthened their determination to practice it.

If we encounter fortunate circumstances, we should never cling to them but should view them as dreams or illusions. If we are prosperous and wealthy, living in a beautiful mansion, we should not think that we are important or great; we should not hoard our wealth or think to acquire an even more splendid residence. We should not be concerned with fame and power. Rather, we should realize that whatever good fortune comes our way is due simply to the kindness of the teacher. Having acquired something valuable or having achieved something great, we should never forget that nothing in this world is permanent. As it is said in the sutras: "What is born will die, what has been gathered will be dispersed, what has been accumulated will be exhausted, and what has been high will be brought low."

In favorable circumstances, we should wish, "May all

the prosperity I now enjoy be distributed to all beings, may it be offered to Guru Rinpoche, and may I myself be content with having just enough food and clothing." To sustain ourselves, in fact, we need only enough clothing to protect us from the elements and only enough food to maintain our lives. We, like the holy beings of the past, should be satisfied with such dwelling places as mountain caves and solitary hermitages.

All the great saints of the past lived in caves, with wild animals as companions, because they had turned from the depths of their being toward the dharma. They based their practice on the ascetic life of a vagabond who has renounced everything. The mind of such a renunciant is ever filled with the dharma, and thought of the dharma leads him to a solitary life in a cave, where his diligence is constantly spurred by the thought of death. We should, as much as possible, adopt this frame of mind as our own.

In this way we can prevent even good situations from creating obstacles to our practice. Otherwise it happens that practitioners of dharma, having achieved some renown, begin to consider themselves teachers or lamas. Thinking in this way, they begin to feel they deserve delicious food, costly clothes, greater fame, and so on. When this happens, grasping and pride becoming strengthened, and the original motivation for the practice of dharma is completely lost. This will not do. By viewing favorable circumstances as dreamlike and illusory, we can avoid such pitfalls and fortify our practice.

We can view the changing states of our practice in a similar way. If we encounter difficulty in the practice itself, such as dullness, wild thoughts, or poor visualization, we should use it as an opportunity to cultivate pure perception. This means the perception of our environment and the beings in it not as ordinary, but as the Glorious Copper-Colored Mountain, inhabited by ḍākas and ḍākinīs. It also means the perception of all appearances as Guru Rinpoche, all sounds as the resonance of his mantra, and all thoughts as the play of his wisdom.

If we encounter the good fortune of very clear awareness and good experiences in our practice we should not think, "Aha! I have become someone really advanced. I ought to be a teacher!" Rather we should not give much importance to it, and we should rest in a fresh and vivid awareness of the present moment, having neither aims nor attachments.

In short, whatever we attain or acquire in the way of wealth, prosperity, fame, food, clothing, or spiritual experiences should never be allowed to generate clinging or attachment within us. Should these feelings arise, we must sit quietly, expel the stale breath three times—thinking that with it attachment, hatred, and ignorance are expelled—and remember how essenceless and fleeting these ephemeral achievements are.

In the distant past, Lord Buddha appeared in the supreme land of India and attained perfect enlightenment. In many places there he turned the wheel of the dharma, enabling many thousands of arhats to achieve realization. Such realized beings could travel in the sky and display many other miraculous powers. Today, nothing at all is left of these marvels except the mere names of the places where they happened. Later, the dharma was brought to Tibet, where it quickly took root and spread, producing many great saints, who in turn transmitted many great teachings. Today, all of these great ones have gone to other celestial fields, and there is nothing left of them here on earth. Remembering this, we must realize that in whatever we might obtain or achieve there is neither substance nor essence. We should never crave either worldly things or dharmic accomplishments and should remain completely free from clinging.

From time to time we may, in reality or in our dreams, encounter violent influences or negative forces coming from wild spirits and troublemakers. If these things happen, we should never, even in dreams, think to annihilate such harmful spirits. We should instead reflect that all these creators of obstacles have in fact been our kind parents in our past lives. Though at one time our father and mother who nurtured and cared for us, they now are intent on causing us injury and harm. The reason for this must be sought and found in negative actions performed in our own past lives. We should further understand that if such negative forces harm us, it is also because they themselves are acting under the poisonous influence of their own negative karma, and in so doing they are creating the causes of future suffering for themselves. Thinking this, we should generate great compassion for them.

If they seem bent on harming us, we should interpret it as an opportunity to purify our own obscurations. All illnesses and hindrances, sicknesses of the body, and sufferings of the mind can be used as the path if we simply see them as being the display of the wisdom of our guru. In this way we can purify our negative karma as well as the sufferings resulting from it. If we maintain this kind of attitude, such negative forces will not be able to create any real obstacles. But if we instead perceive them as enemies, thinking that we must destroy them, we will only make matters worse.

These days, as a result of wild and wandering thoughts, many people experience various kinds of negative disturbances that are merely products of their own minds. If they were to understand such experiences as gifts of the guru by which they can make progress on the path, instead of misconstruing them as outer influences, and if they were to supplicate the guru one-pointedly while generating great compassion for the demons they perceive, then they would be protected from all harm.

If we are troubled by experiences with such negative energies, we should investigate the nature of their apparent existence. We should determine whether or not there is anything concrete or tangible there, something we can grab with our hands or hit with a stick. If such negative energies exist, then where are they located, where do they originate, and what causes and conditions enabled them to arise? With such an analysis in mind, we should recite the Vajra Guru mantra with one-pointed concentration, thinking, "May these spirits encounter only good and beneficial teachings through the great compassion of Guru Rinpoche, and may they bring harm neither to themselves nor to others. May the precious *bodhicitta* take birth in their hearts."

It is especially beneficial to blend the perception of these spirits, our own mind, and the enlightened mind of Guru Rinpoche into one with great compassion. When we understand all appearances to be the display of the wisdom of the guru, then even the word "obstacle" will vanish.

No matter what happens to us, we must always maintain purity of vision, perceiving all phenomena as completely pure and never permitting our minds to stray into conceiving them as the slightest bit impure. We must always see the place where we are as the paradise of the glorious Copper-Colored Mountain and all the beings there, whether tiny insects or our friends and relatives, as ḍākas and ḍākinīs. All we hear must be regarded as the ceaseless sound of the Vajra Guru mantra.

When sitting, we should think of the guru above our head and direct our constant devotion to him. When walking, we should always feel that Guru Rinpoche and his buddha-field are just above our right shoulder and that we are respectfully circumambulating him. We should develop the thought that there is not merely one paradise of the Copper-Colored Mountain, but that within each pore of Guru Rinpoche's body exist billions of paradises with Guru Rinpoche and his retinue in each one.

Before we eat or drink anything, we should first consider it transformed into pure nectar, amṛita, and offer the first portion to the guru residing in our throat. Then we should consider that what we eat or drink—the remnants of our offering—has been given to us as a blessing in order that we might sustain our life. We will in this way eliminate any clinging to or craving for food.

At night, before sleep, we should think that Guru Rinpoche, who has throughout the day been dwelling above of our head, now enters our head and slowly descends to our heart, coming to rest seated upon a luminous red lotus whose four petals are slightly opened. This lotus is very bright, translucent, and vivid. Guru Rinpoche then emanates boundless rays of light, which, having completely illuminated our body and our room, expand and fill the universe with radiance and light. When the entire universe has thus been transformed into pure light, we rest in simplicity, preserving the nature of awareness. Then, just at the moment when we feel ourselves slipping into sleep, we should see the outer universe of light dissolve into ourselves. We, in turn, then melt into light and dissolve into Guru Rinpoche, who himself, now the size of our thumb, melts into light and dissolves into space. Then we should just rest in equanimity in the vast, absolute expanse of void-luminosity. Since falling asleep and death are very similar processes, this practice is particularly important to prepare ourselves for the time of death.

If we awaken and find ourselves unable to retain this luminosity during the course of the night, we should pray fervently to Guru Rinpoche, saying, "May I be able to perceive the luminosity!" Resting in simplicity, we should then return to sleep. If our minds are restless and our thoughts become wild, preventing us from falling asleep, we should realize that these thoughts have neither origination nor dwelling place nor cessation. If we are untroubled by thoughts, we should simply rest undistractedly in the natural state. Should dreams arise, we should try to recognize during the dream that we are dreaming.

In the morning, as we awake, we should see displayed in the sky before us the vast array of Guru Rinpoche and his retinue. All the ḍākas and ḍākinīs who surround him are calling us out of sleep by filling all of space with the sound of the Vajra Guru mantra and celestial music. When we rise from bed, we should think that we are stepping into the celestial field of Sangdopalri. All who dwell there are dākas and ḍākinis, and we ourselves are Vajrayoginī, an unfabricated reality present from beginningless time.

We call out to the guru with yearning and devotion, "Lama Kyeno, Lama Kyeno!"—"You, the guru, you know, you know!" Guru Rinpoche has been dwelling at the red lotus at our heart center; now this lotus opens wide and he emerges, rising to dwell once more above our head. We ceaselessly entreat him, saying, "May my mind be turned to the dharma, may my dharma progress along the path, and may all delusory appearances be transmuted into wisdom."

We should cultivate this practice until our mind is constantly filled with the recollection of the guru. Whatever our activity, whether eating, sleeping, walking, or sitting, the thought of the guru should always be vividly present. One cannot attain accomplishment merely by thus having met the teacher and having obtained some brief advice. The guru is not only to be found externally, but is always present within the enlightened nature of our mind.

Guru Rinpoche said, "I am never apart from those with devotion." If we think that the guru is an ordinary being of flesh and bone, it will be quite difficult to generate the intensity of devotion necessary for progress. Thus we should perceive the guru as embodying the immutable wisdom of Guru Rinpoche, the Lotus-Born, whose omniscience pervades the three worlds and who knows precisely who is praying to him at the moment of their prayer, even if millions of beings are praying at the same instant.

Devotion is the essence of the path, and if we have in mind nothing but the guru and feel nothing but fervent devotion, whatever occurs is perceived as his blessing. If we simply practice with this constantly present devotion, this is prayer itself.

When all thoughts are imbued with devotion to the guru, there is a natural confidence that this will take care of whatever may happen. All forms are the guru, all sounds are prayer, and all gross and subtle thoughts arise as devotion. Everything is spontaneously liberated in the absolute nature, like knots tied in the sky. This is the supreme guru yoga, in which the guru is realized as the indivisible three kāyas. This will be accomplished without having to rely upon rituals of the development stage, without having to rely upon dark retreat, void visions, or the holding of the breath and its entering into the central channel. Through this practice alone, all other practices simply merge into one-pointed devotion, as happened with Gyalwa Götsangpa and other great saints who remained in a state of single-minded devotion day and night, for months and years, letting time flow by and not even noticing hunger and thirst.

Through this devotion, feeling nothing but revulsion toward the attractions of this life, one does not stray into worldly affairs. Acquiring a fine judgment regarding the way actions bear fruit, one does not stray into negative actions. All aspirations to attain peace for oneself alone having ended, one does not stray into the lower paths. Seeing all phenomena as deities, sounds, and great bliss, one does not stray into ordinary perceptions. Seeing all things as the guru, with all one's thoughts enveloped in fervent devotion, one does not stray into negative views. In this way renunciation and a total absence of distraction arise naturally, all that should be abandoned disappears by itself, meditation and postmeditation blend into one, and the true nature of the absolute, one's own wisdom awareness, becomes manifest.

We should continuously practice pure vision until we naturally see that the universe and all beings are completely pure and perfect. Particularly, whether the movements of our mind are directed toward outer phenomena or are gathering internal impressions, we should recognize their nature and let them be spontaneously liberated. We should avoid indulgence in active memories of past activities, cutting through them as they arise. If left unchecked, thoughts such as remembering victories over enemies or savoring schemes that yielded wealth, or any thought of repeating in the future what gained worldly success in the past, will engender a proliferation of thoughts, just as wind over a lake creates ceaseless ripples. If we lose ourselves in memories of situations involving desire, hatred, pride, and jealousy, then we chain ourselves more securely to delusion. It is through preoccupation with these kinds of situations that karma develops and suffering ensues.

When a thought arises, we must simply note that it has occurred, while at the same time remembering that it has come from nowhere, dwells nowhere, and goes nowhere, leaving no trace of its passage, just as a bird, in its course across the sky, leaves no mark of its flight. In this way, when thoughts arise, we can liberate them into the absolute expanse. When thoughts do not arise, we should rest in the open simplicity of the natural state.

In short, no matter what activity we engage in, we should never be apart from the vivid recollection of Guru Rinpoche. Great benefit results from this. In addition, all of our activities should be consciously directed and dedicated toward the benefit of all sentient beings throughout the vast universe. This thought of others is the first point, the basic preparation for the development of the precious bodhicitta.

In the context of the main practice, all of our actions should be illuminated with the realization of emptiness, and our minds should be fixed one-pointedly on the practice itself. This is the second point. If, for whatever reason, it is difficult or impossible for us to generate the realization of emptiness at this early stage in our practice, then we should concentrate with great diligence upon Guru Rinpoche himself, preventing our minds from entertaining even the slightest negative emotion.

Finally, and this is the third point, we should conclude all that we do with a dedication of merit, consciously offering any merit accumulated through our practice and our other positive actions to the benefit of all sentient beings.

These are known as the three supreme points of the great vehicle: the preparation, which will allow our practice to achieve its ultimate fruit; the main part, which will protect our practice from obstacles and deviations; and the conclusion or dedication, which ensures a limitless increase to the benefits of our practice.

If we have developed the ability to focus the mind, then we should find little or no difficulty in practicing this guru yoga. But if we have failed to train the mind properly and have not cultivated the qualities of the path of the great vehicle, and instead insist that we are only willing to practice the Dzogpa Chenpo, or Great Perfection, it will not help us. The view of Dzogchen is quite lofty, while at this time our stream of being is quite low. A child two or three years of age lacks the experience, faculties, and understanding enjoyed by a mature person of twenty. If throughout all of our lives we remember the instructions of the guru, then he will never abandon us, and gradually there will develop in us a sound realizaion of the various stages of the path.

To ensure that the guru always remain with us, we must practice constantly. It is of little benefit to think that a few months or a year of practice will be all that is necessary for attainment. We should practice from this moment until we draw our final breath. Such diligence is necessary if we are to gain the confidence to maintain our faith and our understanding at the difficult and terrifying moment of death. We must ask ourselves if, when death finally comes for us, we will be able to remember all the guru's instructions. Even if we can remember them, it might be quite difficult actually to put them into practice when we are afflicted with the suffering of death, unless we have prepared ourselves by a lifetime spent in constant practice.

A dharma practitioner should be able to cope with all possible circumstances, neither elated by the good nor cast into despair by the bad. In either case, free from expectation and doubt, one should remember the guru. Happiness and sorrow, joy and suffering, though nothing in themselves, can become either a help or a hindrance on the path.

What we ourselves make of these experiences is the test of the genuineness of our practice. This is the true essence of this guru yoga and is itself the main practice. If we practice this to the best of our ability, then there is no other so-called "profound" teaching.

The visualizations of *kyerim*, or the development stage, are of four types, if practiced in a very elaborate way. They correspond to the purification of the four types of birth: birth from an egg, birth from a womb, birth from warmth and moisture, and miraculous birth. But this guru yoga is the essence of all these and requires no such detailed elaboration. All the other aspects of kyerim practice are also included within guru yoga, although they are not considered individually. These are "clear appearance," which is the clear visualization of the deity; "pure mindfulness," which refers to knowledge of all the symbols and aspects of the deity (one head, for instance, symbolizing the oneness of the absolute nature, and two hands, symbolizing means and wisdom); and "firm pride," which refers to the complete confidence and conviction that one has, from beginningless time, always been the deity.

It is said that if we just visualize our root guru with great clarity and vividness for an instant, it is of greater benefit than meditating upon a hundred thousand other deities. This guru yoga is also the quintessence of the *dzogrim*, or completion stage. In *dzogrim*, we find the six yogas: *tummo*, or inner heat, which is the root of the path; *gyulu*, or illusory body, which is the foundation of the path; *milam*, or dream yoga, which is the measure of progress on the path; *ösel*, or luminosity, which is the essence of the path; *bardo*, or intermediate state, which is the invitation to continue on the path; and *phowa*, or transference of consciousness, which allows one to traverse the remainder of the path.

All these practices must unfold within the sphere of guru yoga. The inner heat and illusory body practices correspond to the yoga of the vajra or adamantine body of the guru; dream and luminosity practices correspond to the yoga of the vajra speech of the guru; the bardo and phowa correspond to the yoga of the vajra mind of the guru. This is why guru yoga is also the quintessence of the completion stage practice.

If we aspire to the realization of vast perspective or deeper insight, it is said:

> The realization of your inherent wisdom is the fruit of accumulations, purifications, and the blessings of a realized master. You should know that it is senseless to rely on any other method.

It is also said:

> Whoever wants to find the wisdom beyond intellect without praying to his guru is like someone waiting for the sun to shine in a cave facing north. He will never realize appearances and his mind to be one.

As guru yoga is the ultimate method of realizing the natural state of all things, it is, as stated in the text, "the core of the natural state." By the term "core" we mean the hidden essence, which may not be evident but is at the heart of everything. There are countless instructions for the development, completion, and Great Perfection stages, but they all exist in condensed form within guru yoga. Guru yoga is like the vital link in a chain to which all other instructions are tied. It is a practice that is easy to undertake, has no real difficulties or risk of deviation, and will lead to supreme fruition. As a skillfully devised machine can accomplish in one hour the work of hundreds of laborers, here a single instruction gathers all the others within itself; no instruction, no matter how profound, is excluded. Guru yoga is the main method for furthering progress in our practice and for dispelling all hindrances. It is the "one which accomplishes all."

Technically, guru yoga is part of the so called preliminary practices, but in fact it is the heart of the main practice. Within all the different schools of the Buddhist teachings, be they Nyingma, Sakya, Kagyu, or Geluk, there is not a single path that does not take guru yoga as its main foundation.

In the Sakya tradition, we find the well-known teaching of Lamdre, the simultaneous practice of "path and fruition." There, too, we would begin with the practice of the "profound path of guru yoga." In that instruction, we would receive the blessing or initiation of the body, speech, and mind of the guru and then would meditate upon him. Again, the Kagyu lineage is also known to be heir to the practice of fervent devotion. To engage in the practice of dharma without devotion is to be like someone without a head. No matter how much we may practice the different branches of the path, if we lack devotion, that respectful fervor for the teacher which allows us to see him as a true buddha, then there is no chance for experiences and realizations to arise within us.

The great Kadampa teacher Gyalse Ngulchu Thogme had no other main practice but to meditate on seeing his teacher, the Lord Atīśa, as the true buddha, and to serve him with body, speech, and mind his whole life. In the most famous instruction of the Kadampa lineage, *The Seven Points of Mind Training,* the first step is the practice of guru yoga. Throughout all the different lineages of the Kama,[41] or oral transmission, and Terma, or revealed treasure transmission, the same is true for the Nyingma tradition. There is no path or practice that does not begin by establishing itself within the sphere of guru yoga.

Unlike the practices of the development and completion stages, guru yoga can be practiced at all times. If, for instance, we are practicing kyerim and dzogrim, there are many crucial points concerning bodily posture, speech, and mind that must be observed. In kyerim, when doing a retreat, we must divide our practice into four sessions at specific times throughout the day, and we must arrange an altar with the outer offerings of water, flowers, incense, and so forth, as well as the inner offerings of torma, rakta, and amṛita. But guru yoga can be practiced at any time, under any circumstances, and yet it brings all the accomplishments of the development stage.

In dzogrim, or the completion stage, the practice of the inner heat and the cultivation of various physical exercises such as the great vase and the retention of breath present risks of hindrance and deviation, especially the risk of intensification of the heart *lung,* or "heart energy," and the subsequent disturbance of the mind that such intensification can produce. The practice of guru yoga, on the other hand, involves no such danger, and through it the various *lung*s will enter naturally into the central channel. Just as the eating of food dispels hunger immediately, the practice of guru yoga will generate the realization of the inherent wisdom in us.

When sleeping, when waking, when walking or working or engaging in any kind of activity, we should invoke the guru, thinking, "Lama, you know. Please look on me with kindness." If we always maintain such yearning and devotion, then our mind will become suitable for the teacher's blessings. As it is said, "When the mind becomes fit, the guru does not dwell outside." Our mind has become fit if, having listened to a teacher and relying on him, we always remember clearly what is to be avoided and what is to be adopted and maintain constant vigilance over our actions, words, and thoughts. Armed with this knowledge, we should be determined, even while dreaming, never to perform even the slightest negative action. At the same time, we should cultivate even the most minor positive actions, for just as a large container placed under a trickle of water is filled in very little time, so we can make rapid progress on the path by such attention to positive actions. If we fail to develop this kind of fit mind or mindfulness, we are likely to succumb to the force of bad habits and negative inclinations and thus will tend to ignore what is positive.

We must also develop a capacity for "vigilant introspection," through which we are constantly aware of our activities from morning till night. In this way, if we recognize that we have engaged in negative actions, we should think, "Look at me! I have received so many teachings from my kind guru and yet I still fall back into negative actions. I should feel embarrassed in his presence. All the ḍākas and ḍākinīs must be quite discouraged with me." We should then make a clear, heartfelt confession and generate an unshakable intention to engage only in positive actions from that moment on. If we have been able to accumulate positive actions during the course of the day, we should always remember to reinforce them through the three supreme points or ideas: the preparation or generation of bodhicitta, which here is the intention to act on behalf of all sentient beings; the main part, or the realization of emptiness combined with one-pointed concentration; and the conclusion, in which any merit or benefit accruing from our actions is dedicated to the swift liberation of all beings.

From our discussion of these points, we can see that mindfulness and vigilant introspection constitute the inner guru and the true root guru. It is not someone like me, dressed in robes, sleeping on a throne! If we perpetually maintain such mindfulness and vigilance, we will accumulate positive actions and discard negative ones without difficulty.

Guru yoga is the essence of the eighty-four thousand teachings of the dharma. There is nothing more profound and nothing more vast. All of you, fortunate disciples, should cherish this practice in your hearts. Even when you reach the age of eighty, you should be like Patrul Rinpoche, who every morning without fail aroused devotion through the practice of this guru yoga. Jamyang Khyentse Wangpo had a thorough knowledge of the eight chariots of accomplishment.[42] He not only possessed knowledge of them, but had also practiced all of them. However, his main practice was this guru yoga of the Longchen Nyingthig. He prayed to Guru Rinpoche constantly. Thinking that this guru yoga, though very easy to practice and experience, was at the same time a most extraordinary and profound practice, he unfailingly taught it to his students.

There may be very high practices, like *trekchö* and *thögal*[43] in the Dzogpa Chenpo, but for us to practice these at this point would be like giving solid food to a very young baby. He would not be able to assimilate such food, and it would just cause him harm. If we were to try now to practice those advanced teachings, they would just be wasted. Through the blessings that come from genuine endeavor in the practice of this guru yoga, on the other hand, the realization of Dzogpa Chenpo will arise by itself from the depths of our being like the morning sun, and the meaning of the practice of trekchö and thögal will dawn within us. We should not think that because this guru yoga practice is short it is a minor practice, as though the guru were just giving us a few morsels of food. It is not; it is the most essential practice of all. As Jigme Lingpa himself says in this text, "This guru yoga opens the door to the sky treasury of this essential terma." It arose from the vast expanse of the realization of Jigme Lingpa. If we have confidence in him, we should also have confidence in this guru yoga. Without such confidence, any other profound teaching, such as the Yeshe Lama,[44] will be of no help. If you practice the guru yoga one-pointedly and refuse to fall into the error of viewing it as a minor practice, then the highest realization will dawn on its own.

This guru yoga is referred to as an "outer practice," but this is in no way a deprecatory term. For example, speech and mind depend on the "outer envelope" of the human body, without which any progress on the path would be quite difficult. Similarly, guru yoga encompasses the whole path. These days people seem to think that they should look for a more "advanced" practice. They should remember that the greatest of teachers took this guru yoga as their main practice throughout their lives.

If we practice kyerim, as we have already mentioned, we have to visualize clearly, we have to remember the symbolism, and we must have the vajra confidence that we are the deity. In addition, we must attend to the different aspects of the recitation: *nyenpa*, "approaching"; *drupa*, "accomplishing"; and *drupchen*, "great accomplishment." We must persevere for months and years, accumulating many hundreds of thousands of recitations, before we can reap the fruit of the practice. Beyond this are also the four activities.[45] If all of these aspects are not performed in a perfectly authentic way, then the ordinary and supreme accomplishments cannot be achieved through kyerim.

In dzogrim, too, we must endeavor for a long time in practices that are not without danger if not practiced correctly. But in guru yoga, if we have the ring of faith, the hook of the guru's compassion and wisdom will easily take us to ultimate realization.

It is Guru Rinpoche himself who granted this guru yoga practice. As it is said in the prophecies of the Longchen Nyingthig, "From within the palace of the central channel, the Guru Pema Thötrengtsal will grant this instruction, bestowing his blessing in a symbolic way."

The "palace of the central channel" is the luminosity of mind-as-such, while "Pema Thötrengtsal" means "Lotus Strength of the Skull Garland." Lotus is Guru Rinpoche's name, and the garland of skulls that he wears represents the death of all deluded thoughts and the victory of total awareness. This passage from the text also means that the inner realization of Jigme Lingpa had become equal to that of Guru Rinpoche.

As we have seen earlier, the prophecy related to the Longchen Nyingthig clearly indicates that all beings who make a connection with these teachings and practices—particularly this guru yoga and also the Rigdzin Düpa, the main guru sādhana—will reach the celestial fields of the Copper-Colored Mountain. We should have firm confidence in this and practice one-pointedly. If we practice in this way for, say, one year, and yet experience no extraordinary realization, we should not be discouraged, nor should we succumb to doubts about the practice. As Jetsun Milarepa said, "Do not entertain hopes for an immediate realization, but practice all your life."

If we think with complete determination, "I will practice until my body is taken to the cemetery," then all the experiences and realizations of the path will arise naturally. If, on the other hand, we practice for only a short time, with impatience, then these experiences will not occur. As it is said, "The dharma has no owner except those who persevere in it." If one has the determination to practice the dharma, it is there, ready to be practiced.

Notes

1. *Saṃsāra:* The endless round of birth and death, including this present life, which is pervaded with suffering.
2. A *tertön* (*gter-ston*) or "treasure discoverer" is an emanation of Guru Padmasambhava or of some of the disciples to whom he gave empowerments and instructions in Tibet or other places. Each time he then entrusted one of his disciples to be the holder of a particular teaching and made the prediction regarding the future rebirth of the disciple and the conditions under which he or she would discover these teachings. Guru Rinpoche would thus conceal the teaching, in the form of a symbolic ḍākinī script, in rocks, lakes, and so on, and entrust a protector to guard it. Later, when the time had come for these teachings to benefit beings, the tertön would have visions or signs telling him how to discover the teaching. In the case of "Mind-Treasure," the teachings are not physically unearthed but arise in the tertön's mind by the blessing of Guru Rinpoche. The first tertön was Sangye Lama (1000?–1080?), and the five "kinglike" tertöns were Nyangral Nyima Öser (1124–1192), Guru Chöwang (1212–1270), Dorje Lingpa (1346–1405), Pema Lingpa (1450–?), and Pema Ösel Do-nga Lingpa (Jamyang Khyentse Wangpo, 1820–1892).
3. Rigdzin Jigme Lingpa (1729–1798) was an emanation of Mahāpaṇḍita Vimalamitra, King Trisong Detsen, Gyalse Lharje, and Ngari Panchen Pema Wangyal (see note 9), as well as the immediate reembodiment of Rigdzin Chöje Lingpa, also known as Dakpo Rogje Lingpa (1682–1725). His manifestation in this world was prophesied by the great

tertöns Guru Chöwang (1212–1270), Sangye Lingpa (1340–1396), Chöling, and others.

In childhood he had many visions of saints of the past. At the age of six he entered the monastery of Palgi Riwo, the "Glorious Mountain," and received the name Pema Khyentse Öser. At the age of thirteen he met his root guru, Rigdzin Thekchog Dorje, who gave him the quintessential maturing instructions. In later life Jigme Lingpa had numerous visions of his guru. He also received instructions on the Kama and Terma traditions from many other teachers. Without arduous study he was able, due to his inner realization, to assimilate and express the whole of the Buddhist doctrine. At the age of twenty-eight he did a three-year retreat in the hermitage of Thigle Nyakchik, the "Sole Essence," near Palri Monastery, taking as his main practice of Drolthik Shitro of Drodul Lingpa, and he had many signs of accomplishment. While he was meditating upon Hayagrīva, the horse on Hayagrīva's head neighed, and Guru Rinpoche appeared to him and gave him the name Pema Wangchen. He then had the visions in which the spiritual treasure of the Longchen Nyingthig was revealed to him. As described on page 8, he did another three-year retreat in the Flower Cave at Chimphu, above Samye. After this, following a vision and prediction of Tsele Natsok Rangdrol (1608–?), he went to Tsering Jong, not far from the tomb of King Songtsen Gampo at Chongye, and established there the hermitage of Pema Ösel Thekchog Chöling, where countless disciples were to come from all over Tibet and the neighboring countries. His chief disciples, Jigme Trinle Öser, Jigme Gyalwe Nyugu, Jigme Kundrol, Jigme Gocha, and others, spread his teachings to the borders of China, Bhutan, and India.

By the power of his compassion and prayers, Jigme Lingpa's Longchen Nyingthig was to become, and still is in our day, one of the most widely practiced teachings. His cycle of rediscovered terma teachings and his other writings are collected in nine volumes. Among these is the Yönten Rinpoche Dzö, in which is condensed the essence of the Buddhist path. At the age of seventy, having fulfilled all his aspirations to benefit beings and the doctrine, he left this world for the buddha-field of Lotus Light, amid wondrous signs. His immediate reembodiments were Jamyang Khyentse Wangpo (1820–1892), the emanation of his body; Patrul Rinpoche Orgyen Jigme Chökyi Wangpo (1808–1887), the emanation of his speech; and Do Khyentse Yeshe Dorje (1800–?), the emanation of his mind. There were five main emanations of Jamyang Khyentse Wangpo and Do Khyentse combined, out of whom Jamyang Khyentse Chökyi Lodrö (1893–1959) and H. H. Dilgo Khyentse Rinpoche have displayed ceaseless and all-encompassing activity for the sake of beings and the doctrine.

4. Urgyen (Tib. O-rgyan): The Second Buddha, Guru Pemajungne (Tib. Pad-ma 'Byung-gnas; Skt. Padmākara or Padmasambhava), the "Lotus-Born Guru" who in accord with the prediction of Lord Buddha Śākyamuni emanated from the heart center of the Buddha Amitābha and appeared miraculously upon a lotus in the form of an eight-year-old child. He taught all the nine vehicles, including the various tantras, which Lord Buddha had taught only very rarely and at the ordinary level.
5. Yeshe Tsogyal (Tib. Ye-shes mtsho-rgyal): The princess from Karchen, emanation of Jetsun Drolma, who became Guru Rinpoche's foremost disciple and consort. She wrote down most of the teachings of Guru Rinpoche that were to be concealed as termas.
6. Palri Thekchogling (Tib. dPal-ri theg-mchog-gling): A monastery founded by Tertön Trengpo Sherap Öser (1517–?) at Chongye, in the valley of Yarlung (southeast of Samye in central Tibet).
7. The hundred peaceful and wrathful deities (Tib. Zhi-khro dam-pa rigs-rgya) represent the pure aspects of ordinary inner and outer phenomena and perception. For example, the five aggregates (form, feeling, etc.) are the male buddhas of the five families, and the five elements (earth, water, etc.) are the female buddhas of the five families.
8. Jampal She-nyen (Skt. Mañjuśrīmitra): The lineage of the

Great Perfection, or Ati Yoga, originates with the primordial buddha, Samantabhadra, and then continues with Vajrasattva, Garab Dorje—the first human guru—and Jampal Shenyen. Following a prediction given in a vision by Mañjuśrī, Jampal She-nyen went to meet his guru, Garab Dorje, and attended him for seventy-five years. When Garab Dorje achieved the *body of light* and disappeared into the sky, and as Jampal She-nyen lamented in great despair, Garab Dorje's hand appeared again in the sky and let fall to Jampal Shenyen a casket containing the pith instructions of the "Three Words That Strike to the Vital Point" (Tib. Tshigs gsum gnad rdegs). Jampal She-nyen was the master of Śrī Siṃha, who in turn was the master of Guru Padmasambhava and Vimalamitra.

9. Ngari Panchen Pema Wangyal (1487–1542) (Tib. mNgá-ris panchen pad-ma dbang-rgyal): One of the five tertön emanations of King Trisong Detsen. He was also the author of the famed *Domsum Namnge* (Tib. *sDom gsum rnam nges*), which explains the three vows of the prātimokṣa, the bodhisattva, and the secret mantra, and how they interrelate.
10. Dorje Drolö (Tib. rDo-rje gro-lod): On various occasions, Guru Padmasambhava manifested in eight different aspects, known as the Guru Tsen Gye (Gu-ru mtshan brgyad). Among these, Guru Dorje Drolö, usually riding upon a tigress, is a wrathful form that Guru Rinpoche manifested when subduing negative forces and when hiding innumerable spiritual treasures at Paro Taktsang and other places.
11. Damchen Dorje Lekpa (Tib. Dam-can rdo-rje legs-pa): With Mamo Ekajaṭī and Rāhula, Damchen Dorje Lekpa is one of the three main protectors of the Nyingma tradition.
12. Yidam (Tib. *yi-dam*): Among the three roots—lama, yidam, and khandro—the yidam, or tutelary deity, is the root of spiritual accomplishment. It can be a peaceful or wrathful deity surrounded or not by a mandala and a retinue, upon which one meditates. Its symbolism is explained in the related practices. The verse spoken by Damchen Dorje Lekpa is a verse of the "Sampa Lhundrup" prayer, the prayer of the

"Spontaneous Fulfillment of All Aspirations," found in terma by Rigdzin Gödem.

13. Glorious Copper-Colored Mountain (Tib. Sangdopalri [Zang mdog dpal ri]): The celestial field of Guru Padmasambhava, on the subcontinent of Ngayap, in the southwestern direction.

14. Jarungkashor (Tib. Bya-rung bka'-shor): The famous stupa built in Nepal by a poultry woman and her four sons to shelter some relics of the Buddha Kāśyapa (see *The Legend of the Great Stupa*). These four sons, by the strength of the prayers they made after the completion of the work, were to be reborn as Guru Padmasambhava, the abbot Śāntarakṣita, King Trisong Detsen, and Ba Mi Trisher (a Buddhist minister).

15. Ḍākinī (Tib. khandro [mkha-'gro]) is the feminine aspect, representing the wisdom of voidness. Literally, *khandro* means "sky-goer," and it indicates moving in the sky of the expanse of wisdom.

16. King Trisong Detsen (790–844) (Tib. Khri-srong ldeu-btsan): The great dharma king who invited from India the abbot Śāntarakṣita (Tib. Shiwatso)—also known as Khanchen Bodhisatto—and Guru Padmasambhava to build the monastery of Samye and establish Buddhism in Tibet. He then invited one hundred and eight great Indian paṇḍitas, led by Vimalamitra, to translate all the Buddhist scriptures into Tibetan, together with the same number of Tibetan paṇḍitas led by Vairocana. With the other of the twenty-five main disciples of Guru Rinpoche he received the first empowerment given by Guru Rinpoche in Tibet, at Samye Chimphu. Later, he took successive rebirths as many great saints and tertöns, among them Rigdzin Jigme Lingpa himself and Jamyang Khyentse Wangpo.

17. Samantabhadra (Tib. Kun-tu bzang-po): The primordial buddha who, when manifestation arose from the primordial ground, became a buddha by recognizing this arising to be none other than the display of his own nature. Thus he did not become a buddha through accumulating merit and wisdom—i.e., through cause and circumstance.

18. Rāhula (Tib. gZa'): See note 11.
19. The Great Compassionate One (Tib. Thugs-rje chen-po): A general name for Chenrezik (Tib. sPyan ras gzigs; Skt. Avalokiteśvara), the buddha of compassion.
20. Samye (Tib. bSam-yas): The first monastery built in Tibet, by Guru Padmasambhava, where the Buddhist canonical scriptures were translated into Tibetan and where Guru Rinpoche gave many profound teachings and initiations.
21. Kunkhyen Longchen Rabjam (1308–1363) (Tib. Kun-mkhyen klong-chen rab-'byams): The most eminent of all Nyingmapa scholars and saints, who was the first to put into writing the meanings of the seventeen tantras of the Ati Yoga (rDzogs-chen rgyud bcu-bdun), in his famed *Seven Treasuries* (*mDzod-bdun*), which also contain a thorough exposition of the nine yānas. In visions he met Guru Rinpoche and Khandro Yeshe Tsogyal, and he himself attained the level of the primordial buddha Samantabhadra.
22. Vimalamitra (Tib. Dri-me she-nyen [Dri-med bshes-bsnyen]): The great Indian paṇḍita, emanation of Mañjuśrī, the buddha of wisdom, and disciple of Śrī Siṃha and Jñānasūtra. He came to Tibet, displayed countless miracles, and led the Indian paṇḍitas who participated in the translation of the Buddhist canon. His transmission of the Dzogchen teachings, the Vima Nyingthig, was entrusted to Nyang Wen Tingdzin Zangpo (Nyang-wen ting-'dzin bzang-po).
23. Drati Rikpe Dorje, the "mad yogi of Kongpo" (Tib. bKra-ti rig-pa'i rdo-rje): An emanation of Gelong Namkhe Nyingpo (Nam-mkha'i snying-po), one of the foremost among Guru Rinpoche's twenty-five disciples. He was a close disciple of Jigme Lingpa. He also requested that Jigme Lingpa compose the famed prayer of the "Ground, Path and Fruition" of the Great Perfection.
24. The Great Perfection (Tib. rDzogs-pa chen-po): The ninth and ultimate vehicle. It refers to the primordial purity of all phenomena and the spontaneous presence of the Buddha's qualities in all beings. It is called Great Perfection because all phenomena are included in this primal perfection. There

are three main lineages for the Great Perfection: the Khandro Nyingthig (mKha-'gro snying-thig), which came from Guru Rinpoche; the Vima Nyingthig (Bi-ma snying-thig), which came through Vimalamitra; and the Vairo Nyingthig (Bai-ro snying-thig), which came through Vairocana.

25. Channels: The subtle veins (Tib. *rtsa*), in which circulate the various energies (*rlung*) of the body, energies that carry along these veins the white and red essences (*thig-le*). In the deluded state these three are related to the three poisons, attachment, hatred, and ignorance; in the wisdom state they are related to the three kāyas (see note 29).

26. The seven-point posture of Vairocana (Tib. *rNam-snang chos bdun*):
    (1) The legs should be crossed in the *vajrāsana* posture, the right one over the left.
    (2) The hands, closed into fists, with the thumb pressing the base of the fourth finger, are placed on the thighs at the juncture with the pelvis and the elbows are then locked straight. (Two variations of this are to place the hands palms up, right over left, on the lap, with elbows bent out to the sides, or to place both hands palms down, relaxed, on the knees.)
    (3) The shoulders should be raised and rolled slightly forward.
    (4) The spine should be kept straight, "like a pile of golden coins."
    (5) The chin should be tucked in slightly toward the throat.
    (6) The tip of the tongue should be curled up to touch the palate.
    (7) The eyes should be kept unwaveringly focused at a distance of twelve finger-breadths ahead of the tip of the nose, without blinking.

27. Water with eight qualities (Tib. *chu yan-lag brgyad ldan*): Water that is cool, sweet, light, soft, clear, pure, and that neither upsets the stomach nor irritates the throat.

28. The eight consciousnesses:
    (1) The undetermined and amorphous ground conscious-

ness, already obscured by ignorance, but undetermined with respect to virtue and nonvirtue.

(2–6) The consciousness associated with each of the five sense organs.

(7) Mind consciousness or intellectual cognition of the senses.

(8) Intellection, which is predominantly tainted by the negative emotions (Skt. kleśas).

The first six do not accumulate karma, while the last two do.

29. The kāyas: Various aspects or states of buddhahood. One recognizes two, three, four, or five *kāya*s.

Two kāyas: *dharmakāya,* the absolute body, and *rūpakāya,* the body of form.

Three kāyas: the dharmakāya, or absolute body; the sambhogakāya, or body of divine enjoyment; and the nirmāṇakāya, or manifested body. These correspond to the mind, speech, and body of an enlightened buddha and are expressed as the five wisdoms.

Four kāyas: the *svabhāvikakāya,* or essential body, is to be added to the three kāyas and represents their inseparability.

Five kāyas: to the three kāyas one adds the *avikāravajrakāya,* "unchanging vajra body," and the *abhisambodhikāya,* "body of total enlightenment."

30. Schools and lineages: The first eight are known as the "eight chariots of the lineage of accomplishment," while the ninth one, Geluk, is also known as the Kadam Sarpa, the New Kadam. Details about these eight chariots can be found in the collection of the *Damnga Dzö* (Tib. *gDams-ngag mdzod*), where the main instructions of these eight lineages have been collected by Jamgön Kongtrul Lodrö Thaye ('Jamgon kong-sprul blo-gros mtha'-yas) into eighteen volumes.

31. "Land of the Noble One" (Skt. Āryāvarta) refers to India, so called because it was there that the Buddha lived and achieved enlightenment.

32. *Tīrthika* literally means "those abiding on the river banks," as many of the Hindu ascetics either live near the banks of

the holy rivers or often go there on pilgrimage. By extension this term refers to an adherent of any doctrine other than Buddha-dharma.

33. The three vows (Tib. *sdom gsum*):
    (1) The *prātimokṣa* vows concern all the lay and monastic precepts of conduct taught by Lord Buddha in the Vinaya.
    (2) The *bodhisattva* vows are in essence the wish to generate, cultivate, and preserve the vow to dedicate all one's thoughts, words, and actions solely to the benefit of others. Relatively, this means the exercise of loving-kindness, compassion, and the six *pāramitās*, ultimately leading all beings to complete enlightenment.
    (3) The *samaya* vows are the sacramental links created when a disciple attends a spiritual master and receives from him an initiation. Although it is said that there are one hundred thousand samayas in the Mantrayāna, they can be condensed into the samayas related to the body, speech, and mind of the guru.
34. *Bardo* or "intermediate state" commonly refers to the state and lapse of time occurring between death and the next rebirth. More precisely, one can recognize six bardos: the bardo of birth and life, of meditative concentration, of dream, of the instant of death, of the absolute nature, and of seeking a new existence.
35. Śrāvakas and pratyekabuddhas, the "listeners" and "those who become buddhas by themselves," form the saṅgha or community of the Hīnayāna.
36. The three places or planes are in the sky, on the earth, and below the earth.
37. Here, as elsewhere, the root verses have been amplified by the commentary given by H. H. Dilgo Khyentse Rinpoche.
38. The five buddha families: The dharmakāya, the absolute state, expresses itself as the five wisdoms and five buddha families—buddha, vajra, ratna, padma, and karma—of the sambhogakāya, the subtle body of divine enjoyment. This

sambhogakāya is fully perceived only by enlightened buddhas and partly by the bodhisattvas dwelling on one of the ten levels or bhūmis.

39. The twelve branches of the teaching:

(1) *mdo-sde* (pron. *dodey*): the corpus of the sutras in which the *condensed* (*mdor-bsdus*) meaning is arranged in *sections* (*sde*).

(2) *dbyangs-bsnyad* (pron. *yang nye*): in which teachings formerly expounded in a very detailed way and in prose are now *told* (*bsnyad*) in versified *songs* (*dbyangs*).

(3) *lung-bstan* (pron. *lungten*): in which *predictions* are given regarding future times.

(4) *tshigs-bcad* (pron. *tsikchey*): which are initially written in *verse*.

(5) *chad-du brjod-pa* (pron. *chetu jöpa*): teachings that were *expounded* (*brjod-pa*) *purposely* (*chad-du*) for the sake of preserving the doctrine, without there having been anyone in particular who requested them.

(6) *gleng-gzhi* (pron. *lengshi*): in which elaborate teachings are given on the *basis* (*gzhi* of a *discourse* (*gleng*) that had been given as a precept following some improper action committed by someone.

(7) *rtogs-brjod* (pron. *tokjö*): in which *anecdotes* are retold by the Buddha about contemporary deeds done by others.

(8) *de lta-bu byung-ba* (pron. *detabu jungwa*): Meaning *so it happened*, in which are related stories of the past.

(9) *skye-rabs* (pron. *kyerap*): in which are related the *series* (*rabs*) of past *births* (*skye*) of Lord Buddha as various bodhisattvas.

(10) *shin-tu rgyas-pa* (pron. *shintu gyepa*): in which the vast and profound teachings are expounded in an *extremely detailed* way.

(11) *rmad-byung* (pron. *mejung*): in which are expounded *wondrous* and extraordinary teachings never before disclosed.

(12) *gtan la dbab-pa* (pron. *tenla papa*): in which the mean-

ing of the Vinaya and the sutras is *established* with precision through the classifications (*rab-dbye*) of the aggregates, elements, subjects and objects of perception, and other dharmas of saṃsāra; the description (*rnam-bzhag*) of the stages, path, *samādhis*, and other dharmas of the path; the enumeration (*rnam-grangs*) of the kāyas, wisdoms, and other dharmas of the fruition.

40. Five kāyas: See note 29.
41. Kama (Tib. bKa'-ma): The long oral transmission, which has come down unbroken since the time of Guru Rinpoche. It contains the main practices, initiations, instructions, and commentaries of the Nyingma tradition. It was first assembled into a collection of teachings by Minling Terchen Gyurme Dorje (also known as Rigdzin Terdak Lingpa; Tib. Rig-'dzin gter-bdag gling-pa [1646–1714]), the great tertön and founder of Mindroling (Tib. smin grol gling) and has been transmitted as such down to our own times. It is referred to as the *long* lineage, in comparison with the *short*, or direct, lineage of the Terma.
42. See note 30.
43. *Trekchö* and *thögal* (Tib. *khregs-chod* and *thod-rgal*): The practices of cutting through the solidity of clinging and of direct vision, these two relating respectively to primordial purity (*ka-dag*) and spontaneous accomplishment (*lhun-drup*).
44. *Yeshe Lama* (Tib. *Ye-shes bla-ma*): The teachings from the Longchen Nyingthig which expound the *trekchö* and *thögal* practices.
45. Four activities (Tib. *las bzhi*): Pacifying, increasing, mastering, and wrathful subjugation (*zhi*, *rgyas*, *dbang*, and *drag*).

Acknowledgments

These teachings were given by H. H. Khyentse Rinpoche in spring 1985 at Shechen Tennyi Dargyeling Monastery, Kathmandu, Nepal, at the request of Daniel Staffler and Chris and Constance Gianniotis, to clarify their practice. The teachings were given along with the abhiṣekas for the complete cycle of the Longchen Nyingthig, which His Holiness was giving at Shechen Monastery.

We would like to thank all our dharma friends who so generously collaborated in transcribing and editing these teachings. The recorded translation was transcribed by S. Lhamo and edited roughly by the translator and finely by Michael and Phyllis Friedman, Ani Ngawang Chödrön, Daniel Staffler, and Larry Mermelstein.